Make Learning MEANINGFUL

How to Leverage the Brain's Natural Learning Cycle in K–8 Classrooms

Kristen Vincent

Center for Responsive Schools, Inc.

All net proceeds from the sale of this book support the work of Center for Responsive Schools, Inc., a not-for-profit educational organization and the developer of the *Responsive Classroom*® approach to teaching.

The stories in this book are all based on real events. However, to respect students' privacy, names and many identifying characteristics of students and situations have been changed.

© 2021 by Center for Responsive Schools, Inc.

All rights reserved. No part of this book may be reproduced in any form or by any electronic or mechanical means, including information storage and retrieval systems, without permission in writing from the publisher, except by a reviewer, who may quote brief passages in a review.

ISBN: 978-1-950317-16-5
Library of Congress Control Number: On file

Photographs by Jeff Woodward

Center for Responsive Schools, Inc.
85 Avenue A, P.O. Box 718
Turners Falls, MA 01376-0718

800-360-6332
www.crslearn.org

Contents

Acknowledgments	v
Preface	vii

PART I — 1

- Chapter 1 Introduction to the Natural Learning Cycle — 3
- Chapter 2 The Three Phases of the Natural Learning Cycle — 11
- Chapter 3 Preparing to Leverage the Natural Learning Cycle — 21
- Chapter 4 The Role of Teacher Language — 31

PART II — 39

- Chapter 5 Academics — 41
- Chapter 6 Discipline — 53
- Chapter 7 Social and Emotional Learning — 65
- Chapter 8 Conclusion — 79

Appendix	80
References	91
Suggested Readings	94

Acknowledgments

I would like to first acknowledge the work of Ruth Charney, Chip Wood, and Paula Denton. As founders of Northeast Foundation for Children, which later became Center for Responsive Schools, they laid the foundation for my knowledge and understanding of how students can best find success in school and in life. Their writing and teaching prompted many natural learning cycles of my own as an elementary classroom teacher, professional development presenter, and author.

Thank you to my colleagues, whom I am also lucky enough to call friends. Every conversation and email exchange with you helped me construct many of the ideas shared in this book. I would like to especially thank Deanna Ross and Mike Anderson. Thank you also to Suzy Ghosh, who took the time to answer my call for help in the fall of 2020 as she was embarking on her own unprecedented year as a classroom teacher.

Thank you to Amy Hildenbrand, who first reached out to me about this book concept. Thank you to Clara-Christina Gerstner for her research and literature review, which answered my guiding questions about learning cycles and the brain. She provided the foundational information to launch the writing of this book.

Michelle Gill provided essential feedback as a reader for this book. I am grateful for her insights and questions, which helped bring clarity to many areas of the text. Her perspectives as a classroom teacher, administrator, and educational thought leader were invaluable.

Thank you to the design team at CRS Publishing for their creative vision, which has brought this book to life. I am grateful to the rest of the talented team at CRS Publishing, as well as the wonderful staff of the Marketing department at CRS, as it is often "all hands on deck" to complete a new project.

Deep appreciation goes to both Kevin Bradley, Project Editor, and Emily Hemingway, Editor in Chief at CRS Publishing. Your patience, support, encouragement, and smiles kept me going when I didn't think I had something to say. Your insightful reflections and thoughtful questions guided me through my own natural learning cycle. I am grateful for the strong, positive relationship and trust that we forged during a year of virtual meetings. Thank you for your consistent presence throughout this entire process.

Finally, thank you to my daughter, my biggest supporter and motivator. I have watched her engage in countless natural learning cycles during the past fifteen years. Each day with her is a gift of insight and inspiration.

Preface

The natural learning cycle is not a new strategy or practice in education. Your students have most likely been engaging in the natural learning cycle since birth. However, when children begin their formal schooling, usually around the age of five, the natural learning cycle is often replaced with other teacher-directed models of instruction. The result is often that natural curiosity and exploration are diminished as students complete curriculum work assigned by an adult, with learning goals created by someone else.

With this in mind, I wrote this book to serve as a guide for how you can structure the classroom environment and provide learning opportunities for students to engage in the natural learning cycle while achieving the goals and learning targets of your grade-level curriculum. The natural learning cycle can be used with any prescribed curriculum or learning goals that direct your work with students. It can also be used in every school, with every student, regardless of a school's ranking. For example, students in high-poverty and lower-performing schools often experience compliance-based structures for most of their learning, which is not in alignment with what we know all students need for success. Leveraging the natural learning cycle will breathe new life into rote lessons, help students understand the why and how of discipline, and allow students to practice and develop the skills needed to be an active participant in their own learning. When you understand how a student's brain functions to learn new information and skills, you can naturally mirror that process.

This book is presented in two parts. Chapters 1 through 4 describe the natural learning cycle and the conditions in which it can best be leveraged. Chapter 1 sets the stage for learning about the natural learning cycle by defining it and examining the process as it relates to the functioning of the brain and the foundational ideas of Responsive Classroom that connect to the natural learning cycle. Chapter 2 looks at the background and research, and shares practices, strategies, and activities for successfully engaging students in each of the three phases. Chapter 3 examines practices and strategies that will help educators prepare students to engage successfully in the natural learning cycle, including knowing your students well and creating a positive learning community. Chapter 4 discusses the role of teacher language that will help students feel safe to take risks and allow you to individualize your guidance and support to match each student's needs. By setting expectations and practicing essential routines and skills, you can enable students to build independence and confidence in exploring their own ideas for learning.

The second half of the book, Chapters 5 through 7, shares examples of what the natural learning cycle looks and sounds like for teaching academics, discipline, and social-emotional learning in grades K–8. Chapter 5 provides guidance on teaching academic skills and content using the natural learning cycle, and Chapter 6 shows teachers how to use the natural learning cycle to teach discipline and discipline-related skills. Chapter 7 covers teaching social and emotional skills with the natural learning cycle. Some of the examples presented in the second half were written to highlight a specific phase of the natural learning cycle, while others share about the natural learning cycle from beginning to end. My hope is that these examples provide inspiration for you to consider how best to leverage the natural learning cycle with your own students.

Chapter 8, the conclusion, is a summary of the information shared about the natural learning cycle and offers advice to educators as they begin to leverage the natural learning cycle with students. This chapter is then followed by the appendices and a list of suggested titles for further reading.

I encourage you to engage in your own natural learning cycle while you read this book. Use the reflection questions and prompts to stay connected to your own feelings as you conceptualize how to use the natural learning cycle with students. It may feel uncomfortable or even scary to think about giving over some control to your students and having them make mistakes, but that's where the magic happens. The natural learning cycle includes a structure for students to go back and try again, and to not give up. This will ultimately help your students feel more comfortable about making mistakes, which leads to developing their muscle of intrinsic motivation.

PART I

The natural learning cycle consists of goal setting, working, and reflection. This three-part cycle mirrors how the brain is wired to learn from experience. It is a structure that fosters purposeful inquiry and engagement needed for students' academic and social-emotional learning.

Before using this framework with students, it is helpful to set the conditions needed for it to be most effective. Thoughtful preparation will help things go smoothly for everyone. Knowing your students well, fostering positive relationships, establishing guidelines for routines and behavior, and practicing skills ahead of time will lead to optimal outcomes. Your use of positive teacher language also plays an important role in each phase of the natural learning cycle.

There is no end to education. It is not that you read a book, pass an examination, and finish with education. The whole of life, from the moment you are born to the moment you die, is a process of learning.

—Jiddu Krishnamurti

Introduction to the Natural Learning Cycle

Examples of the natural learning cycle are everywhere. It happens at all ages when we are learning something new or developing a new skill. The developmental milestones of infants and toddlers, such as turning their head to follow sound and movement or learning to crawl and eventually walk, often occur with little direct instruction or intervention. Riding a bicycle, greeting a friend, dribbling a basketball, cooking a new recipe, driving a car, engaging in a friendly conversation, showing empathy, advocating for yourself or someone else—all of these are usually learned by leveraging the natural learning cycle, by following the brain's "natural" path when we teach ourselves something we want to learn. It is a process of learning through experience and reflection.

We refer to this cycle as "natural" because it reflects what we all spontaneously do when teaching ourselves something we really want to learn. When we are in a natural learning cycle, we are actively engaged in exploring and synthesizing information. The result is deeper learning and a lasting change in both knowledge and behavior.

The natural learning cycle consists of three phases. First, we use prior knowledge and experience to determine a learning target. Next, we actively explore new concepts and skills. The learning cycle closes with reflection, to allow time to synthesize new data and determine the next steps or a new direction for more learning.

Research shows that the planning, working, and reflecting cycle provides an optimal sequence for learning (Zull 2002; 2012). We learn best when we can attach a sense of personal relevance to the topic or task. Active interactions that allow for mistakes and self-corrections, and regular opportunities to disengage from activity and reflect upon what we have done, can deepen both engagement and learning.

We Are Hardwired to Learn in Cycles

Young children are learning in cycles in the years before they attend school. Piaget (1923/1959) studied developmental growth by observing young children play. He analyzed how they are able to learn and adopt more and more complex rules that define their play as they grow older. In his explanation of how an individual develops more complex and adaptive skills over time, Piaget characterized learning as a cyclical process, with distinct stages that build on one another.

In exploring learning cycles, researchers have worked to map how information is processed in the brain (Degen 2011; Zull 2002; 2012). In general, information in the brain travels from posterior regions of the brain (back cortex), where sensory and postsensory activity takes place, to anterior regions, in particular the frontal cortex, where more abstract reasoning and knowledge formation takes place:

> The back integrative cortex of the brain is responsible for memory formation and reassembly, integrating sensory information to create images and meaning. When we take time to reflect after learning, we access this part of the brain to develop insights, mentally rerunning and analyzing experiences.
>
> The frontal integrative cortex is responsible for short-term memory, problem-solving, decision-making, assembling plans for action, and making judgments and evaluations. These are skills and actions associated with goal-setting, when we develop plans, and compare and choose options. (Zull 2002, 3–4)

This outline of information processing is not meant to imply that there are no other routes for neuron signaling. In fact, different parts of the brain communicate with each other in many ways. Still, the brain's overarching job is to take in sensory data and generate actions from that data (Zull 2012). This finding supports the concept that learning should be experiential and action oriented.

In the experiential learning process, learners are involved, active, and engaged participants. Students optimally spend most of their school day "doing"—thinking, exploring, and applying what they are learning. Learner participation is central where "learning by doing" is a founding concept (Morris 2019, 4). Students acquire knowledge by processing experiences: "living an experience (digesting, thinking about, reflecting on, and making sense of experience) is the best way for students to acquire knowledge or to consolidate and internalize information in a way that is both meaningful and conceptually coherent for them" (Degen 2011, 19).

The Three Phases

In a school setting, the three phases of the natural learning cycle provide an excellent framework for teaching discipline and rule-following behaviors, social-emotional competencies, and academic concepts and skills. Educational theorists such as John Dewey (1938/1963) and Jean Piaget (1923/1959) were proponents of this three-part cycle, which starts with a goal, leads to an exploration of that goal, and then reflection:

Generating Ideas and Goals. The cycle begins with determining a meaningful goal or sense of purpose that connects to the curriculum and to students' interests and needs.

Actively Working. In the second phase, students actively explore ideas and practice skills, with ample opportunities to dig into materials and ideas, conduct research, solve problems, make discoveries, collaborate, generate new ideas, and then try again.

Reflecting. In the third phase, students reflect on their explorations and practice. What worked and what didn't? What grabbed their attention or presented a new path that could lead to more learning? Questions like these can help students incorporate new experiences into their understanding of how the world works. New or revised goals can begin the cycle again and guide students' continued learning.

This cycle is not always linear. Note that in the illustration the arrows point in both directions between each phase point. Learners are constantly taking in data and making decisions and adjustments as they move through a natural learning cycle. Based on the success during a working phase or on their reflection, students will measure their accomplishment to affirm if a goal has been achieved. If not, they may move back through the natural learning cycle to reset a goal to make it more achievable, or they may make adjustments to the work in order to meet the goal. Or, after some time in the reflection phase, they may decide to put in additional work before reflecting again. It's a fluid process, and can be individualized to each learner and their goals.

A Key to Unlocking Intrinsic Motivation

We teach human beings, not subjects. Our work with students is most effective when lessons focus on the process of learning, not just the teaching of content. In the natural learning cycle, we are also providing students opportunities to experiment, practice, make mistakes, start over after reflection—in other words, to share in the control of their own learning.

We all have innate needs to feel competent, to belong, and to have control and autonomy in our lives. In fact, seeking to meet these needs motivates much of our behavior. When these needs are met, we tend to be more self-motivated and invested in learning; we have higher levels of intrinsic motivation. By contrast, when we feel that we do not have any control or input into our experiences and environments—when we feel incompetent or isolated—we tend to become disengaged, cynical, and alienated.

There are several elements that will help students develop intrinsic motivation when present in lessons and learning opportunities (Anderson 2019, 107; see also Deci 1995; Pink 2009). These elements easily become a part of our lessons when we leverage the natural learning cycle, leading to an increase in student engagement.

Connection. Connecting students to the curriculum and to each other provides a sense of academic and social-emotional belonging. Engaging in learning opportunities together helps students develop essential social-emotional learning skills while learning the grade-level academic content. Teachers use community-building activities to help students get to know each other. Explicitly teaching skills for collaboration, such as cooperation, empathy, responsibility, and problem-solving strategies, is important for successful engagement.

Autonomy. Sharing decision-making with students promotes feelings of power and control. Giving students choices about what and how they learn leads to more self-directed learning. For example, a third grade teacher might invite students to choose how they want to practice math facts by providing options such as spinners, dice, or flash cards.

Purpose. Setting a purpose for learning gives the work a greater sense of significance, especially if the learning is relevant to your students' lives. This allows the work to have meaning beyond the school assignment. Schoolwork then becomes less of an act of compliance in the moment and more about lifelong learning. Communicating to students why they are learning specific content and skills will help connect learning to their own lives outside of the classroom.

Mastery. Allowing for mastery of skills and content gives students opportunities to practice responsibility and take ownership in their learning. Providing time and space for students to use skills on their own or apply the content they have learned in other areas boosts their self-esteem and feelings of competence.

Fun. Elements of fun promote positive engagement, leading to joy. Enjoyment is a powerful driver in motivating students to repeat an experience. Providing an appropriate level of challenge is an important element in bringing joy to learning, as well as crafting lessons that include elements of movement and interaction.

Only a few of these elements need to be present for students to experience an increase in intrinsic motivation, and the natural learning cycle already has many of these elements built right into the structure. The three-part process of the natural learning cycle allows a learner to set a goal or purpose, do the work to meet that goal in ways that make sense to the learner, and reflect on the successes and areas for continued growth, ultimately allowing for mastery of the skill or content. By fostering intrinsic motivation with the natural learning cycle, student learning goes deeper and becomes more lasting.

Your Own Natural Learning Cycle

Are you aware that you are about to begin your own natural learning cycle? Right now, it may feel overwhelming to dig into yet another teacher resource and learn new strategies for delivering instruction. I completely understand those feelings, and I designed this book to be a resource for both new learning and support. I will guide you through each stage of the natural learning cycle and include specific examples and lessons you can use with your own students. I will also provide reflection questions to highlight the natural learning cycle you are experiencing and offer support for you as a learner. Thinking about your own learning of the ideas and strategies offered in this book can help you better use the natural learning cycle with your students.

The *Responsive Classroom* Approach

The ideas and strategies in this book come from *Responsive Classroom*, a student-centered, social-emotional learning approach to teaching and discipline. This evidence-based way of teaching offers practical strategies for bringing together social, emotional, and academic learning throughout the day.

A core belief that guides the practices and strategies of the *Responsive Classroom* approach is that in order to be successful in and out of school, students need to learn a set of social and emotional competencies: cooperation, assertiveness, responsibility, empathy, and self-control (C.A.R.E.S.). According to the Collaborative for Academic, Social, and Emotional Learning (CASEL), a leading organization in the field of education, social and emotional learning is "the process through which children and adults acquire and effectively apply the knowledge, attitudes, and skills necessary to understand and manage emotions, set and achieve positive goals, feel and show empathy for others, establish and maintain positive relationships, and make responsible decisions" (CASEL 2021).

Since 1981, the *Responsive Classroom* approach has provided strategies and resources that raise educators' competencies in four critical domains: offering engaging academics, building a positive community, effectively managing the classroom, and matching instruction to students' developmental strengths and needs. Through use of the natural learning cycle, teachers incorporate *Responsive Classroom* teaching strategies and practices such as knowledge of child development, positive teacher language, rule creation, Interactive Modeling, and Academic Choice.

True teachers are those who use themselves as bridges over which they invite their students to cross; then, having facilitated their crossing, joyfully collapse, encouraging them to create their own.

—Nikos Kazantzakis

The Three Phases of the Natural Learning Cycle

The natural learning cycle is grounded in how our brains are wired to learn from experience. The three-part process of starting with a goal, experimenting and testing ideas, and then reflecting on the outcome is a familiar one to many educators. These three phases allow for the purposeful inquiry and engagement needed for academic and social-emotional success. Students become stakeholders in their own learning.

Start With the Purpose

Before jumping into the first phase of the natural learning cycle, it's important to set a positive tone for learning. This begins with sharing the purpose of the lesson or activity with students. I often hear teachers telling students *what* they are going to learn or practice, but when students hear *why* they are learning about a specific piece of content or practicing a skill, they can make a personal connection to their learning. When learning is connected to students' own lives—their interests, strengths, and prior knowledge—it becomes relevant and more meaningful to them, and as a result fosters motivation. Like adults, students are motivated to accomplish things that matter to them.

My colleague Caitie Meehan, a classroom teacher in Washington, DC, shared the importance of communicating to students why they are learning what they are learning:

> A few years ago, as I looked around the fourth/fifth grade combination class I taught, I saw a student staring at her math notebook and slowly shaking her head. I wandered over to her and said, *"You can always talk to me if something is puzzling you. I might be able to help."*

"It's not the math," she said. *"It's just . . . I like fractions and all, but I don't know why I'm learning this. When will I ever use it?"*

In that second, I realized that I had been so focused on getting the instruction across that I'd forgotten a crucial part of the lesson: the *Why*. I hadn't taken time to help students see that the learning I was asking them to do connected with their daily lives. Without that connection, learning lacks meaning. And without meaning, students often struggle to find the motivation and the energy needed for the hard work of learning. (Meehan 2016)

Phase 1: Generating Ideas and Setting Goals

Taking the time to help each of your students articulate a learning goal for themselves sets a tone of collaboration and mutual respect. It sends the message to your students that their ideas are going to be taken seriously and that they will have a say in what they'll be learning. Goal setting also fosters reflection and self-knowledge by prompting students to ask themselves questions such as "What's important to me about this?" or "What do I want to improve on or learn more about?" Students who create learning-driven goals are developing intrinsic motivation, which is rooted in desire and appreciation for knowledge acquisition. Another way to look at it is that the student is competing with themself, striving to reach their potential (Covington 2000).

After students hear why they are learning something or practicing a skill, it's important to surface what students know and don't know, their strengths and areas for growth. Students will need to realistically self-assess where they are and then decide on a meaningful and realistic goal. For example, a student who might be feeling apprehensive about learning the sevens multiplication facts may state what they already know when expressing their goal: "I've memorized the multiplication facts up to the sixes, so I'm ready to tackle the sevens. I will study them for five minutes each day this week in preparation for the quiz on Friday." Generating new ideas for learning often happens right after students finish reflecting on their work. For example, students may reflect on their own writing by considering what they did well and then choose one thing to focus on improving next time—punctuation, spelling, writing a strong topic sentence or hook, or adding more sensory details.

A goal in the natural learning cycle can be short term or long term. It can be achieved in a twenty-minute practice lesson or worked on during a three-week project. Regardless of the time frame, effective learning goals are specific, attainable, relevant, and well defined. Focusing on these attributes will help students develop goals that provide a clear picture of what they are striving for. In addition, when students develop goals with these characteristics in mind, they will be better able to sustain the motivation and energy needed to achieve it.

Specific goals name a concrete outcome. For example, "This term, I want to learn how to write an effective persuasive essay that convinces my parents to change my weekend curfew" or "My goal is to memorize my sevens multiplication facts by Friday for the quiz." Avoid general goals, such as "I'd like to improve my writing."

Attainable goals are age appropriate and within reach for the student to achieve in the time frame given for the activity or unit of study. For example, a fourth grader interested in chemistry might set a goal to read a grade-level book about Marie Curie or Louis Pasteur for a monthly book report. A seventh grader interested in chemistry might set a goal to learn about the origins of the periodic table of elements in preparation for an upcoming science fair project.

Relevant goals are personally significant and connect to a student's learning in school. If you are working within a set curriculum that determines what students need to learn, you can share the broad goal and then have students set personal goals related to the larger one. For example, if the purpose of the lesson is to practice writing a personal narrative, students could set a personal goal of improving the skillful use of an element of personal narrative, such as starting with a strong hook or using descriptive language that includes vivid details and imagery: "My goal is to include sensory details in my personal narrative by describing how things sound, smell, taste, feel, and look in every scene."

Well-defined goals have an outcome that students are able to visualize. To help them determine if their goal is well defined, ask your students, "How will you know when you've achieved your goal?" If students struggle to answer the question, they should go back and refine the goal, making it more specific, attainable, or relevant. A student is ready to move on to phase 2, the actively working phase, when their goal:

- Names a specific outcome that is age-appropriate and attainable
- Connects to the purpose of the lesson and is relevant to the content, topic, or skill
- Provides a bit of a challenge
- Contains a time frame or deadline

Skillful goal setting takes practice and develops through repeated experience. While setting specific, relevant, and attainable goals may initially be time-consuming for students, it is important to take the time needed to carefully teach them how to set age-appropriate and attainable goals and provide opportunities to practice. Goals will lay the foundation for the rest of the natural learning cycle, so students should become proficient at setting them.

To support students in learning how to set goals, provide sentence stems or fill-in-the-blanks. Here are some examples:

- My goal is to [*discover/learn/practice*] [*specific information/skill*] by [*day/time*].
- This [*term/month/week*], I want to learn _____.
- In this lesson, I hope to learn how to _____.
- Today, I want to practice _____ so that I can _____.
- This week in [*subject area*], I want to discover the answer to _____.

Choose a Challenging Goal

Be sure the goal is not related to a skill the student is already proficient in or is familiar with. The goal should provide a small amount of challenge. It should be a skill the student cannot yet do well, information they do not already know, or a question they don't already have an answer for.

Phase 2: Actively Working

During this second phase, students dig into the work and engage in reading, practicing, exploring, researching, discovering, creating, and experimenting. Students also may be collaborating with others and engaging in problem-solving.

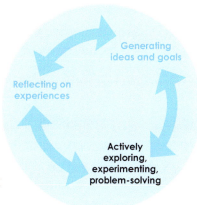

The role of the teacher is essential during this phase. You will set expectations, carefully observe students at work, ask questions, facilitate, and coach.

Setting Expectations

It is important to first set expectations for student work and behavior for this active time. When students know the guidelines, they can be more personally responsible for their own learning and behavior. Feelings of security and predictability are fostered, and there are often fewer disruptions. Students should be more focused on tasks and not be left with questions about what to do or how to do it.

Provide students with time frames. Students need to know how much time they have to spend in the actively working phase and when this phase is expected to end. You will also need to determine and share with students whether the expectation is that they be finished with their work at the end of this phase or if it's OK not to be completed yet. Regardless of this decision, students can still engage in reflection.

Share expectations for positive behavior. Before work begins, connect with your classroom rules. Share specific expectations for behaviors such as voice and noise level in the room, movement around the classroom, cooperation, partnering and collaborating with others, and responsibility for work and materials. For example, one colleague, a second grade teacher, has a voice-level chart posted in her classroom. Before students begin their work, she focuses on the level called "work talk." She reminds her students that this means anyone at your table should be able to hear you but classmates at other tables should not, and conversation should be only about your work and your learning.

Communicate criteria for good work. It's especially useful to create criteria for good work with students. Having clear criteria posted will help build student independence.

Students can also use the criteria to self-assess their work and see if they are accomplishing their goal rather than relying on an adult to do so. To help students see if they are on the right track, share any rubrics, checklists, or anchor charts. (See the appendix, pages 80–84, for examples.)

Observing, Facilitating, Coaching

In their role as coach, teachers show students how to apply what they know in order to achieve their goals. By working individually with each student and adopting a style that is both encouraging and collaborative, we can "help them learn from experiences in their life context" and "assist in the creation of personal development plans and provide ways of getting feedback on performance" (Kolb et al. 2014, 223).

Observe students carefully. Note students who may need additional support—those who are easily distracted, have a hard time getting started, or get quickly frustrated and always seem to seek help. At the same time, make note of students who are focused, seem to enjoy the work, and work independently. Careful observations can help us get to know students and better inform our planning.

Use teacher language for unlocking student success. Skillful use of envisioning, reinforcing, and reminding language and of open-ended questions enables students to think for themselves, self-assess, persevere, and problem-solve. (Chapter 4 is dedicated specifically to teacher language, where we will dig deeper into these types of language.)

What follows are a few suggestions for ways to talk with students during the actively working phase.

> *Check in with students:*
>
> - Reassure those who are on the right track.
>
> - Reinforce those who work to solve problems or ask for feedback.
>
> - Refer back to established criteria so students can engage in self-evaluation. Ask, "How is the work you're doing helping you reach your goal?"

Ask first before offering help:

- If a student is struggling or off track, first ask if they want assistance or direction.

- Remember, it's the student's work, not yours.

- Before offering advice, pause and ask, "Would you like some help with that?" or "Can I offer a suggestion that has helped other fourth graders?"

- If the student says, "Yes," then proceed with a guiding question or a suggestion.

- If the student says, "No, not right now," step back and continue to observe the student. Check in periodically to see how things are progressing.

- If the work is appropriately challenging, the student can learn a lot from working through problems independently.

- If you notice the student is struggling with several aspects of their work and they accept your invitation for assistance, provide just one suggestion at that time. Resist the urge to fix everything all at once.

Facilitate time management. Remind students to stay on topic, and help students set small benchmarks. For example, for students who need assistance, you can break down the work time into steps that the student can check off when completed or check in with you first before moving on. Provide verbal and visual reminders about time. Use countdown timers, and provide five-minute and two-minute warnings as the work time comes to a close.

Teach and model skills in the moment. This could be anything you see a student struggling with, from using a glue stick to technology issues. Taking a few moments to model a skill with a student can go a long way in building their independence and feelings of competence.

A student is ready to move on to the third phase and engage in reflection when they can answer "yes" to the question "Have I reached my learning goal?" You might refer back to established criteria for good work and have students engage in some self-evaluation before reflecting.

While actively working and experience may support learning, it does not always result in learning. We have to include time in lessons and activities for reflection, the third phase: "We have to engage with the experience and reflect on what happened, how it happened and why. Without this, the experience will tend to merge with the background of all the stimulants that assail our senses every day" (Beard and Wilson 2006, 20).

Phase 3: Reflecting

In *A Handbook of Reflective and Experiential Learning: Theory and Practice*, Jennifer Moon suggests that "to reflect on something is to bring it into ownership" (2004, 86). Reflection helps students assimilate and consolidate what they've learned, consider how their actions have influenced the outcome of their work, and generate ideas for new directions for future work. Reflection allows students to see what worked for them and where there might be areas for growth. Reflection allows students to learn more about themselves as learners.

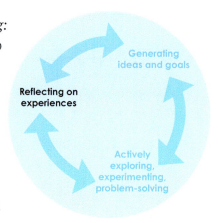

Every student should engage in some type of individual reflection, since each student created their own goal for learning. Reflection can simply be a question that a student silently answers for themself. Reflection can be expressed aloud—in an around-the-circle or classroom format, in a conference with the teacher, or with a partner or small group of classmates. Reflection can also be written—students can jot an answer to one or more reflection questions or complete a reflection sheet that the teacher has prepared.

The use of open-ended reflection questions encourages self-awareness. (See Chapter 4 for more on open-ended questions.) Open-ended questions prompt students to consider the content learned, the skills practiced, or the learning process they engaged with. What follows are examples of reflection questions you might ask.

- What did you learn?
- What is something you know now that you didn't know before?
- What is something you can do now that you couldn't do before?
- What surprised you about your work?

- How did you know you were working toward achieving your goal?
- Did you make any adjustments to your work? What were they? Why did you make them?
- What problems did you encounter while you were working? How did you solve them?
- What might you do differently next time?
- Based on this learning, what else do you want to learn or practice?

A Flexible Cycle

The natural learning cycle's three phases should ideally happen in order, mirroring how our brain functions naturally to learn something new. However, the cycle is designed to accommodate a student moving back to make an adjustment, allowing them to reset a goal or redo some work. In fact, great learning and growth can happen when a student recognizes the need to go back and rewrite a goal or redo some work.

For example, after reflecting, the flexibility of the cycle may be utilized. A student may realize that their original goal was not well defined or specific enough, or the skill that they actually need to practice has changed, entailing the need to reset a goal or redo some work. Or, if multiple small goals are generated for a long-term project, there may be several sessions of working and reflecting before the student moves on to a final reflection phase at the end of the unit of study or project.

Your Own Natural Learning Cycle

You are starting your own natural learning cycle now! I suspect you are probably entering into a goal-setting phase. After reading about the phases of the natural learning cycle, you may have some questions about preparing to use this process of learning or about what type of classroom environment you might need to create. Or you might feel ready to dig more deeply into teacher language. Consider setting a learning goal for yourself now. Look back at the table of contents so you know where we are headed. This can help you generate a goal that is specific and well defined.

Children must be taught how to think, not what to think.

—Margaret Mead

3

Preparing to Leverage the Natural Learning Cycle

At this point in the book, you may be feeling a bit apprehensive and thinking that this framework might not work for your students. This feeling is a common one when learning about a new approach to instruction. You cannot take a new strategy such as the natural learning cycle and just pop it into your lessons and expect it all to go smoothly. Jumping in without thoughtful preparation will produce undesired results and difficulty for everyone involved. Successfully leveraging the natural learning cycle with your students begins with careful, strategic planning and establishing a climate of trust and a positive classroom environment.

Know Your Students Well

Knowing your students is the foundation for crafting successful learning opportunities and experiences. But knowing students well is more than just knowing their names—it is understanding who they are as individuals: their likes and dislikes, passions, strengths, cultures, family structures, and levels of support at home and in the community. It is also important to be aware of each student's social and emotional development, and it can happen in different ways:

> A middle school teacher who sees 150 adolescents for one subject, 45 minutes a day will likely develop different kinds of relationships with their students than a first grade teacher who has one class of 22 six- and seven-year-olds.

> What is likely the same is that each teacher has a unique understanding of (and rapport with) each class—be it from year to year, or block to block. (Center for Responsive Schools 2018a)

Understanding key social and emotional developmental milestones can help inform how we structure each phase of the natural learning cycle. When we recognize our students' general abilities for working independently and in groups, their levels of tolerance for making mistakes, and their capacity for accurate self-evaluation, we can better meet students where they are, leading to deeper learning. The table that follows shares some key social and emotional characteristics at each age.

Age	Social and Emotional Developmental Characteristics
5	• Want adult approval • Like to help, cooperate, follow rules • Respond to clear and simple explanations • Can sit and work at quiet activities for fifteen to twenty minutes at a time, particularly tasks with manipulatives
6	• Ambitious; may choose projects that are too hard • Highly competitive • Extremely sensitive; extreme criticism can truly be traumatic • Ready to take on individual and group responsibility
7	• Prefer working alone or with one friend • Upset by changes in room arrangement or scheduling • Rely on adults for help and constant reassurance • Conscientious and serious about schoolwork; don't like taking risks or making mistakes
8	• Love group activities and cooperative work • May prefer working with some classmates more than others • Adjust well to change • Bounce back quickly from mistakes or disappointments
9	• More individualistic • Often feel worried or anxious; easily frustrated • Very critical of self and others • Competitive; can work in groups but with lots of arguing

Age	Social and Emotional Developmental Characteristics
10	• Generally happy and friendly • Basically cooperative and flexible • Do well with group activities and collaborative learning • Appreciate being noticed for their efforts
11	• Need time to talk with peers • Desire to test limits and rules is an important developmental milestone (not a personal attack on teacher) • Inclusion/exclusion issues loom large • Love the challenge of competition
12	• Capable of self-awareness, insight, and empathy • Enthusiastic and spontaneous • Can help peers significantly with schoolwork; will make good use of time allowed for partner and group work • More able to handle long-term assignments
13	• Pay close attention to peers • Worry and complain about schoolwork • Tentative, unwilling to take risks on tough intellectual tasks • Often quieter and more secretive than twelves or fourteens
14	• Learn well in cooperative learning groups • Are in a know-it-all stage • More willing to admit an error and try something a second or third time • Typically loud and rambunctious

Adapted from Chip Wood, *Yardsticks: Child and Adolescent Development Ages 4–14*, 4th ed. (2017).

It's important to get to know the class as a whole as well as each student:

> The individual interests, ages, quirks, abilities, and challenges in the room help to create a whole-class personality. That personality will shift as the students who contribute to it grow and change, both individually and as a group. (Center for Responsive Schools 2018a)

Start to learn your students' social and emotional capabilities at the beginning of a new school year, and be aware of the new characteristics that will appear as students grow older during the school year. Their abilities and attitudes will change, and so too should our instructional approach. As a fourth grade teacher, I saw a big shift in my students during the school year. Nine-year-old students entered my classroom nervous, anxious, critical, and competitive. About six months into the year, as many students turned ten years old, they became more cooperative, eager, enthusiastic, open, and friendly toward just about everyone. It was at that point that I would slowly shift my instruction to include more partner and small-group work, introduce more independent research projects, and hold more whole-class discussions and debates.

Knowing students developmentally, and observing ways in which they change and grow during the school year, can help inform how best to leverage the natural learning cycle. At some ages, students will resist group work, while others will embrace it. Some students will rely on your approval and guidance, and at other times they may relish the opportunity to work independently. Staying aware of these shifting developmental characteristics can help you guide students in finding success in all aspects of their learning.

Foster Positive Relationships

Just as important as knowing our students is building and maintaining positive relationships, which are key for structuring engaging lessons. Teachers who form meaningful relationships with students take the time to learn about their personal goals, interests, and happenings in their lives. Students who feel a connection with their teacher, and with each other, experience increased trust and emotional safety, which can lead to greater academic engagement. Creating a positive learning community begins with students knowing each other and their teacher, and practicing cooperation, understanding, and empathy. What follows are some suggestions for routines and activities that help foster a sense of positive community.

Greetings

Welcoming each other with warmth and respect builds the foundation for a friendly, equitable classroom community. Greetings can foster a sense of belonging and recognition.

- **Welcome at the Door.** Standing by your open classroom door, greet each student by name as they enter the room.

- **Good Morning Circle.** Gather students together in a standing or seated circle. You can begin the greeting by turning to the student on your left and saying, "Good morning, [name]." That student then returns the greeting, saying, "Good morning, [teacher's name]." That student then turns to the classmate on their left and continues the greeting. You can also add in various gestures and handshakes, such as a wave, a high five, or a pinky shake.

Get-to-Know-You Group Activities

Facilitate cooperative games and activities that allow everyone opportunities to participate. This will help foster a positive sense of belonging and acceptance. Be sure to highlight for students what they are learning about each other as they engage in the activity.

- **Just Like Me.** Have students sit in a circle. Start by standing and naming an interest or experience that students may share, such as "I have a pet." Any student who connects with that statement stands up and says, "Just like me!" and then sits back down. Repeat several times with a variety of statements.

- **A Warm Wind Blows.** Set a group of chairs in a circle, with one less chair than the number of students participating. The student without a seat walks to the center of the circle and says, "A warm wind blows for anyone who ____," filling in the blank with a category ("likes ice cream"). Everyone who fits that category comes into the center of the circle and then quickly finds a new place to sit, including the person who started in the middle. The person who doesn't find a seat now stands in the center of the circle and says, "A warm wind blows for anyone who ____," naming a new category. The game continues for several rounds.

- **Take Sides.** Create a list of contrasting statements about students' preferences; for example, "I like to sleep late" and "I like to get up early," or "I like to be with big groups of people" and "I like to be with just one or two friends." Begin with students standing in a line down the middle of a circle area or the classroom. Call out a pair of statements, pointing to opposite sides of the room for each one. Students move to one side or the other to indicate which statement they agree with. Students who are undecided can stay in the middle. Repeat for several rounds.

Create an Optimal Learning Environment

Creating a positive learning environment will help facilitate optimal learning and offer students a safe, engaging classroom community. Here are three useful strategies.

Set guidelines for behavior. When students are invested in the class rules, they are more likely to be intrinsically motivated to contribute to a safe, focused, and enjoyable classroom environment. Connecting rules to student goals helps to build ownership. Students become invested by seeing how rules can help them achieve their goals. For example, you might ask your students, "If we want to learn about dinosaurs [or: how to divide with double-digit numbers or learn about simple electric circuits], what rules might we need to help reach this goal?" Brainstorming positive behaviors proactively sets a tone of cooperation and responsibility.

Practice reflection. Invite your students to practice reflection in an informal way by asking open-ended questions about experiences they've had or behavior you've observed. For example, if you notice that your class walked quietly in a single line from the gymnasium back to the classroom, say, "I noticed our line was quiet and straight all the way back to our classroom. What helped you follow our guidelines today?" After recess, you might ask, "On a scale of 1 to 5, with 5 being awesome, it was so much fun, and 1 being horrible, it wasn't fun at all, how did recess go for you today?" Students respond by holding up the number of fingers that corresponds with their reflections about recess. If you noticed that during some independent work students remained focused and demonstrated stamina, you might say, "You all were all so focused on your work. Did you know you were working productively for twenty-five minutes? How did you do it?"

Promote and foster a growth mindset. Kolb and Kolb (2008, 304) note that a key aspect of metacognitive knowledge is what someone believes about themselves, especially where it concerns their ability to learn: if you don't believe you can learn, you won't. One way to focus on growth is to use the word "yet" when discussing areas for improvement. For example, "This doesn't make sense yet, so let's keep reading to see if we can learn more" or "You haven't mastered the steps of long division yet. Keep using the anchor chart until you have all the steps memorized." Another way is to teach students how their brains can grow and change. JoAnn Deak's *Your Fantastic Elastic Brain: Stretch It, Shape It* is a good introduction to growth mindset. Her picture book shows how the brain can develop with exercise, just like the rest of our bodies. A third way is to use stories and analogies to help make abstract concepts about working smarter, trying again, and not giving up more concrete and accessible for students.

Be sure to be open about your own mistakes in order to build an atmosphere of safety and trust. Show students that we all make mistakes, and that by taking responsibility for them we can turn them into opportunities for new learning.

Teach and Model Essential Routines and Skills

It is best not to assume that students of any age know what is expected of them or are familiar with when and how to use materials, even common school supplies. We need to be explicit about our expectations around routines, skills, and behaviors. Clear, simple, and well-practiced routines create a calm, predictable, and safe environment in which students can do their best work. Taking the time first to model and practice routines and skills will allow students to see the rules in action and to effectively learn what a positive behavior looks like, sounds like, and feels like.

Interactive Modeling. This strategy will teach the procedures and routines to keep the classroom running smoothly and safely. Interactive Modeling gives students an active role and allows them to observe, think about, and then practice a new skill or routine right away. (See the appendix, pages 85–88, for examples.)

Steps for Interactive Modeling

ELEMENTARY K–6

1. Describe what you will model and why.
2. Model the behavior.
3. Ask students what they noticed.
4. Invite one or more students to model the behavior.
5. Again, ask students what they noticed.
6. Have all students practice.
7. Provide feedback.

MIDDLE SCHOOL 6–8

1. Describe what you will model and why.
2. Model while students notice.
3. Give students the opportunity to collaborate and practice.
4. Reinforce their practice with immediate feedback.

Here are some ideas for using Interactive Modeling:

- **Routines.** Explicitly teach routines such as how to gather materials, find an appropriate spot in the room to work independently or with others, and clean up when the working phase is finished.

- **Care for materials.** Teach students ahead of time about materials they might use to accomplish their goals. This might include microscopes, math manipulatives, art supplies, or graphic organizers.

- **Academic skills.** Model and teach the academic skills students may use while engaged in the natural learning cycle. These include the use of technology, how to conduct research, organization strategies, and time management.

Your Own Natural Learning Cycle

You are moving into the working phase of your own natural learning cycle. Consider what you just read in this chapter about setting students up for success. How does this information fit into the goal you set for yourself at the end of Chapter 2? Does it connect to, enhance, or extend your goal? Reflect: What did you read in this chapter that is already a part of the teaching and learning in your classroom, and what strategies might you add to create an optimal learning environment for students to successfully apply the natural learning cycle to achieve their goals?

Language is one of the most powerful tools available to teachers ... and what [students] hear and interpret—the message they get from the teacher—has a huge impact on how they think and act, and ultimately how they learn.

—Paula Denton

The Role of Teacher Language

Teacher language refers to the professional use of words, phrases, tone, and pace to enable students to engage in active, interested learning; be contributing members of a positive learning community; and develop positive behaviors. (Denton 2013, 3). What we say and how we say it plays an important role in each phase of the natural learning cycle. Effective teacher language conveys faith in students' good intentions, and our tone and choice of words can let students know we believe in them and their ability to succeed. A teacher's words can "help students understand how they think and work, giving them insight into what they are capable of and how they can articulate and achieve academic, social and behavioral goals" (Center for Responsive Schools 2016, 3).

There are many types of teacher language that can support students as they learn and grow.

Envisioning Language

Success does not come easily to some students, and schoolwork can often feel difficult. To feel invested in their work and inspired to keep going—even when it's hard—students need a clear and engaging picture of what is possible. Envisioning language helps students see a path to their own potential, and sets a positive tone for future work. Envisioning language paints a clear and enticing picture that helps students see themselves achieving in ways that connect to and go beyond what they already know and can do.

Use envisioning language during the goal-setting phase to help students visualize a successful outcome. When students can see and hear about the possible positive outcome of their efforts, they become more inspired to work toward their goals.

Try . . .

"Good morning, scientists. I am looking forward to helping you discover answers to all the questions you have about outer space and our solar system."

"Writers, you are going to become class experts on personal narratives. Your effort and hard work will help us improve our writing together."

"We're about to set new goals for exploring more complex algebraic problem-solving. Given how well you've done with our earlier work, I believe you have the strategies needed to meet this new challenge with success."

Avoid Overgeneralizations During Goal Setting

"This is going to be really exciting!" How many of us have said this, with the intent to stimulate student interest and excitement about an upcoming lesson or activity? Overgeneralizations such as these are common in our teacher language. However, we don't really know how all our students will feel about the lesson. It's best to avoid overgeneralizations, especially when getting students started with goal setting or while they are actively working. You can still share your feelings about the topic or lesson, but be sure to invite students to form their own opinions.

Instead of . . .	Try . . .
"You're going to love this unit of study!"	"I'm really excited about this next unit of study, and I hope you will be, too."
"That book is so inspiring."	"Some readers have found that book inspiring. I'll be interested to hear what you think."

Reinforcing Language

Students learn best when they have opportunities to build on their strengths. One way we can better help students focus on their strengths is by moving beyond general praise ("Great job") and instead name concrete and specific actions that illustrate what students are doing well. This allows students to know exactly when they are on the right track and what actions and behaviors are contributing to that. Reinforcing language helps students develop an understanding that ability and success are less about being smart, and more about hard work, persistence, and a positive attitude.

Reinforcing language can be used effectively in all three phases.

Instead of . . .	Try . . .
"That's a great goal!"	"This learning goal is specific and clear. I can see that you are really challenging yourself this time."
"Good job with your note taking."	"I see you wrote the main idea in your own words and noted where you found that information."
"We had some nice reflections today."	"I noticed many of you were pausing before sharing your reflections. That shows careful thinking."

Reminding Language

An effective tool to use during the working phase is reminding language. It prompts students to remember expectations they've learned and to make positive decisions based on those expectations. In addition, reminding language can help students get back on track if they've strayed off course. For example, if student voices are too loud during a working period, try saying, "Everyone pause. We agreed to use level-2 voices during this work time, but I hear much louder voices. What are some of the reasons we agreed level 2 would be helpful when we are doing this type of work?" Take some responses from the students, and summarize with saying, "Let's try again, keeping those reasons in mind." Reminding language can also be used proactively before a potential challenge arises: "It's been awhile since we've used the microscopes. What do you remember about handling them safely?" It's important to respond early to signs of off-task behavior. Little behaviors can lead to bigger issues if not addressed right away.

Tips for Using Reminding Language	For Example . . .
Keep reminders brief.	"Before we get started, what meeting rules should we keep in mind and practice?" "Mia, what can you do if you get stuck?"
Phrase the reminder as a question or a statement.	"What are some ways you can make lining up feel safe and friendly?" "Adrianna, remind me what you are supposed to be doing right now."
Avoid: • A teasing, exasperated, angry, or tired tone of voice • Sarcasm • Crossed arms, raised eyebrows	Keep your tone and body language neutral. Respond when you and the student(s) are both calm.

Open-Ended Questions

Questions are an essential part of all three phases of the natural learning cycle. Open-ended questions in particular can be used to support the natural way students learn by promoting engagement and encouraging self-awareness.

Open-ended questions have no single right or wrong answer—any reasoned answer is a good one. By using open-ended questions, we are showing trust in our students' ability to think for themselves, to come up with reasonable ideas, and to contribute in valuable ways to their own learning. As a result, students are likely to develop a stronger sense of autonomy, competence, and belonging—feelings that lead to greater engagement and investment in their learning.

Tips for Using Open-Ended Questions	For Example . . .
Signal that all reasoned and relevant ideas are welcome. Use words such as might, may, could, or possibly.	"What might you do to gather information for your research?" "How could you use additional resources to strengthen your work?"
When discussing academic struggles or behavior challenges, students are more likely to share ideas when they feel their answers do not have to reflect their own personal views or experiences. Use phrases such as "some people" and "some students."	"Why might some students find it difficult to get started right away on their work?" "How do some people handle frustration when the work isn't going according to their plan?"
Encourage multiple perspectives, using words such as how many, different, and other.	"What are some different ways you might share your findings?" "What are other ideas for staying focused in a busy classroom?"
Do you really want to hear what your students think?	If you have one specific answer in mind, ask a closed-ended question or make a statement.

Students' responses to open-ended questions at all three phases of the learning cycle help them develop more sophisticated thinking and knowledge, which leads to even deeper learning.

Generating Ideas and Goals:

What do you wonder about _____?

What might be some ways you can practice _____?

What do you already know about _____?

What might you want to learn more about?

Reflecting:

What surprised you about your work?

What made this work easy/challenging/difficult/frustrating for you?

What would you do differently next time?

What did you learn?

How do you know yourself better as a learner?

Actively Working:

How else could you organize that?

What might help you _____?

What do you think will happen if you _____?

How does this compare with _____?

What's your thinking behind this?

Tone and Intention

Paula Denton notes that "tone conveys an enormous amount about how we're feeling and what we're truly thinking, perhaps even more than our actual words. It can achieve our intended purpose or override it and sour our communication in an instant" (2013, 15). Speaking in an even, warm, matter-of-fact tone shows respect and conveys faith in our students. When we use singsong tones, an angry voice, a loud sigh, or sarcasm, our students may feel confused, humiliated, or resentful—regardless of our intentions—and our communication becomes indirect and dishonest. Over time, students may stop trusting their teacher and no longer feel that the classroom is a safe place. Be aware of your tone when speaking to students, and be sure it communicates your best intentions.

Listening to Students

The key to listening to our students is to talk less: "In our eagerness to guide and inform, we fill the air with our pearls of wisdom when we should be asking our students for their pearls, then listening carefully to what they have to say" (Center for Responsive Schools 2016, 29). Giving our students opportunities to speak deepens their learning, allowing them to better formulate their thinking and remember their learning.

Instead of . . .	Try . . .
Finishing the sentence for a student if they are hesitating or fumbling for words	• Maintaining eye contact • Understanding what the student is saying before formulating a response
Interrupting to correct, elaborate on, or repeat a student's words	• Using wait time, pausing before you reply • Paraphrasing the student's message before adding your own thoughts
Jumping in to help a student who might be struggling	• Ask first before offering help (see also Chapter 2)

Your Own Natural Learning Cycle

Positive teacher language is essential for success with the natural learning cycle. Take time now to reflect on your own teacher language. What felt familiar about what you just read? What is a new idea or skill? What are some steps you might take to make a positive change? Consider the power of your words and how you can ensure they are used in support of your students' learning in all three phases of the natural learning cycle.

PART II

Leveraging the natural learning cycle helps students develop autonomy, intrinsic motivation, and responsibility while increasing their knowledge and skills. The natural learning cycle challenges students to choose a focus for their learning or practice, based on their needs or interests.

In order to give purpose to the learning that occurs during the natural learning cycle, there first needs to be a common foundational experience. This is when we share, teach, and model the skill or content with our students. This could be a direct teaching minilesson, a modeling of a skill, or a role-play of rule-following behaviors.

After this foundational experience, we observe students as they apply the skill or work with the content. We look for areas where students seem to struggle, where there might be gaps, or when students are ready to take that learning to the next level. From those observations, we identify a skill or content knowledge to address the area for growth. This becomes the focus for their work while engaged in the natural learning cycle.

The Natural Learning Cycle Process

1. **Provide a Foundational Experience:** Direct teaching, modeling

2. **Identify Area(s) for Growth:** Academic behaviors, skills, or the content

3. **Leverage the Natural Learning Cycle:** Explore an idea, learn content, practice skills

    Goal setting

    Working

    Reflection

Most people don't aim too high and miss. They aim too low and hit.

—Les Brown

Academics

Students explore, learn, and practice academic content with the natural learning cycle. It provides students with more autonomy and responsibility for the mastery of content and skills. Using the natural learning cycle is a process, so it can have strong outcomes but also feel chaotic and messy. Teachers using the natural learning cycle expect noise and activity in the classroom, along with mistake making and perhaps feelings of frustration. The more you use the natural learning cycle with students, though, the better everyone will become at managing the framework and using it to learn, even when there is failure.

Academic foundational experiences are ones in which we share, teach, and model the academic content and skills. This might be a whole-class minilesson on paragraph structure or CVC words, a modeling of how to use a microscope or paint with watercolors, or an introductory presentation on the branches of government or the water cycle.

The natural learning cycle should not become the only strategy used when teaching academic subjects, nor should it replace other frameworks that are used successfully with your students. The natural learning cycle should be used in addition to many other commonly used structures for teaching and learning. For example, many elementary teachers use the workshop model for teaching writing. The natural learning cycle can be layered into the writing workshop process, with goal setting and reflection happening around the active practice of drafting, editing, and conferencing.

What follows are examples of the natural learning cycle process at different grade levels with different types of academic content and skills.

Grade Level: Kindergarten

Subject: Math

Content/Skill: When given a number less than 10, students can identify the second number needed to total 10.

1. **Provide a Foundational Experience:** Modeling how to count out a set of objects (up to 9), then adding the correct number of objects to make a total of 10.

2. **Identify Areas for Growth:** Working more accurately—keeping work organized to accurately identify the number needed to make 10.

3. **Leverage the Natural Learning Cycle:** One class period.

   Goal setting: To have students work more accurately. Students will decide how to keep track of their work when making 10 (for example, use of manipulatives, drawings, baskets, bins, cups, paper, or whiteboards).

   Working: Students solve "making 10" problems using their own method for keeping their work organized.

   Reflection: How might being more organized help you in math?

Spotlight: The Natural Learning Cycle in Kindergarten

Kindergarten teacher Ms. Lin is beginning an introductory unit on the concept of addition. The focus this week has been for students to practice making the number 10 when given a number from 1 to 9. At the start of each math lesson, Ms. Lin modeled for students how to do this using a variety of math manipulatives. She also modeled how she recorded her answers on a worksheet that contained the set of equations to solve.

During the practice period of the lessons, Ms. Lin observed her students working to make 10. She noticed that several students often miscounted their manipulatives, arriving at an incorrect answer. Some were rushing and others were mixing up different piles of manipulatives, and it seemed that her students could benefit from learning about some organizational strategies to help them to work more accurately. Ms. Lin decided to leverage the natural learning cycle for a lesson on how to stay organized, with the goal of working more accurately to identify the correct number needed to make 10.

Ms. Lin begins the lesson by sharing what she noticed yesterday: "I watched you while you worked on those math problems yesterday, to find numbers that add up to 10. It seemed to me that using the blocks, cubes, tiles, and teddy bear counters helped you with your counting to solve the math problems. I could see your thinking as you counted to make 10. I also noticed that some of you made some mistakes with your answers, which always happens in math. I know sometimes kindergartners count too fast, or get distracted and forget where they are with their counting. Turn to someone next to you and share with them when you might have made a mistake with counting or finding the right answer, and if you can, share why you think that happened." After a few minutes, Ms. Lin raises her hand to stop the partner chat. She then shares the goal for the lesson today: "I thought I would show you today some ways to organize your math work that might help you work more accurately. We'll get a chance to try some of these out today, so be thinking about which idea might work best for you."

Ms. Lin models for her students several organizational strategies using paper, cups, bins, baskets, and whiteboards at the tables and on the floor. She then asks her students to set a goal for themselves while they are working today. She provides a sentence starter: "When I make 10, I will _____ so I can _____." She then provides some examples: "When I make 10, I will use cups for my tiles so I won't get them mixed up. When I make 10, I will use colored papers to keep track of my work so I can count the right number to make 10."

Once students have shared their goal, Ms. Lin invites them to gather their materials as she hands out a worksheet with a new set of problems to solve. Ms. Lin observes as her students work. She uses open-ended questions to check in with them: "I noticed you are using paper, and you divided it into columns. How does that help you keep track of your work?"

After about twelve minutes, Ms. Lin signals that it's time to stop working. She tells students to put everything down and turn their attention toward her. She first shares what she noticed: "You seemed so focused on your math work today. Those twelve minutes flew by! I saw so many new organizational strategies being used today."

Ms. Lin then asks a few reflection questions: "Let's use our thumb gauge. Thumbs up if your organizational strategy worked for you today, thumbs down if it didn't, and thumbs somewhere in the middle if it sort of helped you stay more organized." She scans the room at all the thumbs in the air, and asks, "How might being more organized help you in math?" She takes a few answers from students who raise their hands, and then says to the class, "Now turn to someone next to you and share if you can think of any other times when being organized has helped you." After a brief partner chat, Ms. Lin tells students it's time to clean up and turn in their worksheets.

Grade Level: Second

Subject: Science

Content/Skill: Provide an explanation for why certain plants and animals only live in certain habitat areas.

1. **Provide a Foundational Experience:** Gather research on different habitat areas, such as temperate forest, desert, tropical rain forest, grassland, arctic, and aquatic.

2. **Identify Areas for Growth:** Communicating an explanation or position to others.

3. **Leverage the Natural Learning Cycle:** Two class periods.

    Goal setting: Choose a way to communicate your explanation for why certain plants and animals live only in certain habitat areas. For example, writing, oral report, poster, or narrated PowerPoint slides.

    Working: Students create their communication method (write, rehearse, record, and so on).

    Reflection: How does a method of communication affect an audience's ability to understand your position or explanation?

Spotlight: Teacher Language During the Working Phase

Mr. Ross, seated on the carpet with his second graders, asks if there are any more questions. After several seconds of wait time, he sends the students back to their seats to begin the working phase of their animal research projects. For the next several minutes the classroom bursts with noise and activity as students gather materials. They can be heard asking questions as they check in with each other, negotiating the use of materials or work space, and sharing their plans. A few students hesitate on the carpet so they can first talk one-on-one with Mr. Ross. When he finishes speaking with those students, Mr. Ross turns his attention to the classroom. He observes the students as they settle down to work, noticing who is able to get started right away and who is still wandering around the room. He uses reminding language to prompt these students to get started. "Leighanne, show me the spot where you are going to work today. Dion, remember to gather all your materials now and bring them to your seat first."

After a few minutes, Mr. Ross approaches a table of students using tablets and uses open-ended questions to ask about their work: "Darnell, why did you choose to create PowerPoint slides to communicate your ideas?" Mr. Ross listens, then follows up with another open-ended question: "What is the big idea you want to communicate in your slides?" He reminds Darnell to make sure that big idea is represented in words and graphics.

Mr. Ross walks over to another table and turns his attention to a student leaning over a large piece of poster paper, and asks, "Shanice, how are you going to organize your poster?" He listens carefully, nodding his head as Shanice describes her plan. "Sounds like you've given this a lot of thought! I'll check back in with you to see how it's coming along," Mr. Ross says.

Mr. Ross visits a group of students who are working on the floor and chatting about what they might do outside during lunch recess. He addresses the group, redirecting their attention back to their work: "What are some ideas for staying focused on your work in a busy classroom?" He listens as they share a few strategies. "I'll be looking and listening for those ideas today, so everyone can accomplish the work they have planned," he says.

Grade Level: Fourth

Subject: Writing

Content/Skill: Incorporating description in a personal narrative.

1. **Provide a Foundational Experience:** Direct teaching of the elements of a personal narrative; share examples with anchor texts.

2. **Identify Areas for Growth:** Using more description.

3. **Leverage the Natural Learning Cycle:** Several class periods.

   Goal setting: How might you add more description in your writing? What tools can you use? For example, anchor texts, thesaurus, use of five senses.

   Working: Writing workshop—students use tools to write more description into their personal narrative drafts.

   Reflection: How does a personal narrative change when there is more description? What is the experience like for the reader?

Spotlight: Interactive Modeling During the Goal-Setting Phase

The fourth graders in Mrs. Williams's class are seated at their desks with their writing folders. Mrs. Williams uses her document camera to display a piece of her own writing on the whiteboard. The students are familiar with these paragraphs, because Mrs. Williams showed her students this story yesterday when reviewing elements of a personal narrative. She explains the goal of the work they will engage in for the rest of the week during writing: "For the next few days, we are going to focus on how to add more description to our personal narratives, to really bring these stories to life for our readers. Today, I am going to show you one strategy for adding more description to your personal narratives."

She prompts the students to get ready for an Interactive Modeling lesson by saying, "I'm going to show you how I use my five senses to add some vivid description to my story. Watch carefully when I work, because when I'm finished, I'll ask you about what you noticed." She takes a highlighter and draws a line over a few sentences in her story. She then takes a sticky note and places it near the first sentence she highlighted. She writes the words "see, hear, feel, taste, smell" in a column on the left side of the sticky note. Mrs. Williams then looks as if she is thinking deeply. She jots down some words about the five senses as they relate to the ideas in her sentence. She then rewrites the sentence in her story, adding some of the descriptive words she brainstormed. Mrs. Williams looks up and asks, "What did you notice?" Many students immediately raise their hands and share some details about what Mrs. Williams was doing. She then asks, "What do you think my thinking sounded like in my head?" Mrs. Williams calls on a few more students who speculate about what she was doing.

She then directs her students to take out their own personal narrative drafts and asks them to consider how they might use this brainstorming strategy today. She asks if anyone has found a sentence in their own writing that could use more description, and then asks if anyone would like to come up to the document camera and model the five senses brainstorming strategy that she just shared.

Grade Level: Eighth

Subject: Social Studies

Content/Skill: Explain the historical context and significance of changes to the U.S. Constitution.

1. **Provide a Foundational Experience:** A general study of the Bill of Rights and other amendments to the U.S. Constitution.

2. **Identify Areas for Growth:** Students can only name a few amendments to the U.S. Constitution and are unclear in their understanding. Students should know and understand key, significant, and controversial amendments that have had important roles in past and current events.

3. **Leverage the Natural Learning Cycle:** Five class periods—three for research and two for class discussions.

    Goal setting: Choose an amendment from the list below to research. Share why you want to learn more about it and what you hope to discover.

    - First Amendment: Freedom of religion and speech, and to petition to assemble.

- Fourth Amendment: Protection against illegal search and seizure.

- Fifth Amendment: Protection against self-incrimination and double jeopardy; the right of due process and to a grand jury.

- Sixth Amendment: Right to a speedy and public trial and an impartial jury, and right to counsel.

- Fourteenth Amendment: Granted former slaves citizenship and equal protection; established principle of selective incorporation.

Working: Students conduct research to understand the meaning of the amendment and the historical origins of the amendment. Students will identify a meaningful U.S. Supreme Court case on the amendment and connect the amendment to real-life applications. Students will work in small groups to lead a class discussion on each of the amendments researched.

Reflection: How do these constitutional amendments affect your lives today?

Spotlight: An Active and Interactive Reflection Activity

Mr. Diaz is ready to lead his social studies classes in a reflection activity to wrap up the student research projects on amendments to the U.S. Constitution. Instead of leading a whole-class discussion, Mr. Diaz decides to get his students up and moving while sharing answers to a reflection question.

Mr. Diaz stands at the door and welcomes his first period students into the classroom. He prompts them to read the message on the interactive whiteboard:

Dear Constitutional Amendment Experts,

Today we will reflect on our work last week and everything we learned about the amendments to the U.S. Constitution. To get ready for our work today, there are two tasks for you to complete during arrival time:

1. Think about how you might answer this question: In what ways do the constitutional amendments we studied affect your lives today?

2. Work together with your classmates to carefully move your desks to the edges of the classroom. We need to create a big empty space in the middle of the room.

After the bell rings, Mr. Diaz closes the classroom door and looks around the room, and says, "Looks like there was some good teamwork in here! We have a nice, big empty space for our reflection activity today." He then directs the students to stand in a big circle, so everyone can see each other, and provides instructions for an activity called concentric circles. After counting off by twos, the ones form an inner circle facing the twos and partner with the student across from them.

Mr. Diaz asks the question that was written in the welcome message: "In what ways do the constitutional amendments we studied affect your lives today?" He then encourages partners to share their ideas with each other. After several minutes, Mr. Diaz rings a chime to signal that it is time to stop talking. Students wrap up their conversations and then turn their attention toward him. Mr. Diaz gives directions for the outside circle to move one person to the right, and to share ideas about the same question with this new partner.

After one more round, Mr. Diaz concludes the reflection activity. He directs his students to think about one important or new idea they gained from their conversations as they move their desks back into position. When students are seated, Mr. Diaz asks for volunteers to share aloud any important or new ideas they gained as a result of their reflection conversations.

Your Own Natural Learning Cycle

Think about the curriculum topics you teach, and where you might begin to leverage the natural learning cycle with your students. Consider times when it is more important for students to construct their own knowledge or practice a skill on their own.

Natural Learning Cycle: Academic Reflection

- Think about the projects and lessons you have designed for your students. Jot down some of them here.

- Can some of these projects and lessons be adapted to fit the natural learning cycle? How?

- Can you provide more ownership for students by having them set a goal for themselves at the start? What might that look like and sound like?

- How might you incorporate more reflection, so that students become more responsible for their own learning outcomes, instead of just waiting for a grade or teacher feedback?

Enthusiasm is common.
Endurance is rare.

—Angela Duckworth

Discipline

Discipline is something to be taught. The origin of the word reflects this, coming from the Latin *disciplina*, which can be interpreted to mean education, teaching, and instruction. In school, students are learning how to follow rules. We don't expect students to come to school knowing how to read and write, so we shouldn't make the assumption that students know how to follow the rules. Like any other content area subject, discipline can be learned.

We know that students learn best when actively engaged in constructing their own understanding. Teaching discipline begins with creating a safe, welcoming, and predictable climate, which provides the foundation needed for establishing a positive learning community. To prevent off-task behavior and misbehavior, we establish rules and hold students accountable to those rules in a proactive, firm, fair, and consistent manner. In the same way that students learn the steps for long division, students need to learn the steps for following the rules. The learning steps for both involve modeling, coaching, and repeated practice. Positive reinforcement of what is going well is also key to successfully teaching discipline.

Strong foundational experiences are important when teaching discipline. This is when we establish developmentally appropriate expectations for positive behavior. Foundational experiences for teaching discipline include establishing rules and then using Interactive Modeling to demonstrate what it looks like and sounds like to follow those rules during the school day. (For more on Interactive Modeling, see Chapter 3.) Most classroom rules fall into three categories:

- Taking care of ourselves
- Taking care of others
- Taking care of our classrooms and materials

Role-play and class meetings are other foundational experiences that help establish ways in which students can follow the rules.

Strategies for Exploring Rule-Following Behavior

Class Meetings

A class meeting is a strategy to try when the agreed-on rules are not working, when the problem affects everyone in the class, and when you are open to student input.

1. Choose an appropriate meeting time.
2. Start on a positive note.
3. State the reason for the meeting.
4. Connect the problem to the class rules.
5. Invite students' input with open-ended questions.
6. Ask for potential solutions to the problem.
7. Choose a solution to try.
8. Sum up the plan.
9. Continue to follow up. As students implement the agreed-on plan, reinforce their efforts and recognize their successes. (Center for Responsive Schools 2018b, 107–109)

Role-Play

Role-playing prepares students for more complex social interactions by acting out scenarios that can be handled in many positive ways.

1. Describe a specific situation. Stop at the point where a behavior decision will occur.
2. Name the positive goal.
3. Invite and record students' ideas for a solution.
4. Act out one idea with the teacher in the lead—or "tricky"— role. Audience notices what actors say and do.
5. Ask students what they noticed.
6. Act out another idea, and consider having a student take the lead role. Audience notices what actors say and do.
7. Again, ask students what they noticed.
8. Act out other ideas.
9. Sum up lessons learned.
10. Follow up. Check in with students to see if they are using some of the solutions they practiced and if they are working. (Center for Responsive Schools 2018b, 66–67)

When using the natural learning cycle to teach discipline, there are times when it might be more useful for students to set a goal for the entire school day or even several days instead of for just one activity, subject, or class period. For example, the teacher shares an area for growth and guides students to set a goal for themselves at the start of the school day. Then, the working phase would be taking place all day, whenever that skill might be used. The reflection would happen near the end of the school day. The area for growth becomes a focal point throughout the extended period of time for both teacher and students, reinforced along the way with positive comments and reminders.

What follows are some examples of the natural learning cycle process being used to teach discipline at different grade levels.

Grade Level: First

Rule to Follow: Taking care of yourself and others, the classroom, and materials.

1. **Provide a Foundational Experience:** Rule creation.

2. **Identify Areas for Growth:** Finishing the job of cleaning up.

3. **Leverage the Natural Learning Cycle:** Throughout day during times when cleanup is happening.

   Goal setting: What does it look like and sound like to clean up? How will you know you are finished cleaning up? What specific action will you take today to ensure we have clean, organized learning spaces in our classroom?

   Working: Practice during the school day.

   Reflection: How does a clean workspace/classroom make you feel? How might a clean classroom help you and your classmates? How does it help you follow the rules?

Spotlight: Reflection

Mrs. Rodriguez gathers her students together at the end of the week to reflect on how their cleanup efforts have been going. She begins by saying to the class, "This week, we have been working on doing a better job at cleaning up. Let's think about how we've done with that. Show me fist to five. A closed fist means zero, meaning you think we did not do a good job with cleaning up, and five means we did a great job with cleaning up this week. Show me with your fingers how you think we did as a class with cleaning up this week." Mrs. Rodriguez looks around at her students to see how many fingers they are holding up. "I see lots of fours and fives, and a few threes. Looks like there was some improvement with cleaning up." She tells her students they can put their hands down and then asks, "I am wondering if anyone has an example of cleaning up that they'd like to share about." She listens as a few students share. Mrs. Rodriguez then asks, "How does a clean, organized classroom make you feel? Turn to a classmate and tell them." After several minutes, she ends the reflection by asking her first graders to think to themselves about one way they can continue to do a good job cleaning up next week.

Grade Level: Third

Rule to Follow: Taking care of others.

1. **Provide a Foundational Experience:** Modeling expectations for respectful talk.

2. **Identify Areas for Growth:** Asking questions respectfully.

3. **Leverage the Natural Learning Cycle:** Throughout the day.

    Goal setting: We've been working on using kind words and talking respectfully to each other. Now we want to focus on asking questions in a respectful way. Or, when we're angry or frustrated, use a statement instead. Share an anchor chart with strategies. Set a goal today for using one of these strategies.

    Working: All day.

    Reflection: Did anyone try these strategies? How did it feel? Was anyone asked a question that seemed more respectful today? What made it respectful? How did it feel? How might respectful questions help us in our learning? And help us follow the rules?

Spotlight: Goal Setting

Ms. Jackson set aside some time in the morning to launch a natural learning cycle lesson for the day with her third grade students. She gathers the students together on the carpet and says, "We've been working on using kind words and talking respectfully to each other. That's one way we can follow our class rule about taking care of others. I heard more friendly tones and words this week. Kind words are one way you can help take care of each other. Today, I want to focus on asking questions in a kind and respectful way. I've noticed sometimes that I hear questions asked in loud, frustrated tones, or questions that sound bossy or demanding. Questions are a great way to learn more about each other or to ask for help. However, if you are angry or frustrated, making a statement would be a better strategy." Ms. Jackson reveals an anchor chart, and reviews it with the students.

Ms. Jackson shares verbal examples and models for students what pieces of the anchor chart information look like and sound like. She has students turn to a classmate and practice the appropriate tone of voice, and then she has them stand up to practice appropriate body language. She reinforces the idea that if you ask a question in a loud, rude, or condescending tone, the other person may feel accused of doing something wrong. In that case, you should just simply tell the other person why you are upset or what is bothering you.

Ms. Jackson asks her students to set a goal for themselves for the day: use one or a few of the strategies from the anchor chart when asking questions. Ms. Jackson asks students to raise their hands for each of the items on the anchor chart and share what goals they set for themselves. She tells students that she will be watching and listening, and everyone else should do the same, too. She lets students know that they will reflect together at the end of the day. Ms. Jackson then dismisses the students back to their desks to get ready for math.

Asking Questions

Tone of Voice:

- Kind, friendly
- Calm
- Voice rises

Body Language:

- Hands open, at your side
- Eye contact
- Safe distance away— arm's length

If you feel angry, frustrated, or upset, make a statement to share how you feel.

Grade Level: Fifth

Rule to Follow: Taking care of yourself and others.

1. **Provide a Foundational Experience:** Use role-play to practice strategies for how to communicate and handle frustration.

2. **Identify Areas for Growth:** Communicating and handling frustration in group work.

3. **Leverage the Natural Learning Cycle:** Throughout the week.

   Goal setting: What are some appropriate ways of handling your frustration during group work? It's appropriate when it helps you calm down and at the same time takes care of other group members. It involves using a straightforward, respectful tone and words ("I statements"), and strategies to calm down and that allow you to rejoin the group. Choose one idea you can try this week when we have group work.

   Working: All week, when engaged in group work.

   Reflection: What worked for you? What might you try differently? How can we support classmates who are trying new ideas to handle frustration during group work? How does communicating frustration in a way that takes care of yourself and others help us follow our classroom rules?

Spotlight: The Working Phase

Mr. Miller directs his fifth graders to gather together in their community action project groups. Students pack up materials at their desks and gather in groups of four or five in designated areas around the classroom. Mr. Miller watches for a few minutes as students settle into chairs and spots on the floor. He rings a chime, and when all students are quiet and looking in his direction, he reminds them of the goals they set for the week about using strategies to handle frustration when working in groups. He asks students to share any success they've had so far in using any of the strategies they've been practicing. A few students share about experiences from yesterday. Mr. Miller asks students to think quietly to themselves about a strategy they might use today. He asks for a thumbs-up from everyone when they've decided on a strategy to try, and then lets the fifth graders know they have twenty minutes for working in their groups today.

The groups start working on their plans to organize and run an upcoming community service campaign. Mr. Miller walks around the classroom, watching and listening to the groups work on their community action service projects. Mr. Miller is listening for tones of frustration, anger, or disagreement to see if students are employing the "I statements" and other strategies they have been working on. Mr. Miller makes a point of approaching each group, asking open-ended questions to prompt some new thinking or to help move a group along if they seem stuck. He asks, "How did you decide on these plans you have written down so far? How have you resolved any disagreements? Is every group member's voice represented in these plans?" Mr. Miller uses reminding language to help draw students' attention to the strategies they have been working on. With one group, Mr. Miller models how to use an "I statement" instead of staying quiet when there is a disagreement.

I Statement

I feel/felt _____ when I see/saw (hear/heard) _____ because _____.

Example: I felt angry when I saw you sitting in my seat in the cafeteria because I couldn't sit next to my friends.

Grade Level: Seventh

Rule to Follow: Taking care of others.

1. **Provide a Foundational Experience:** Class meeting—using respectful words and tone, even when there is a disagreement or frustration.

2. **Identify Areas for Growth:** Moving beyond "I liked it" or "good job." Offering specific, positive feedback on classmates' work.

3. **Leverage the Natural Learning Cycle:** One class period.

    Goal setting: What is useful about feedback? How you can give a classmate helpful feedback about what you like about their work? What makes the work good or high quality? How do you communicate that?

    Working: During English class—feedback on essays.

    Reflection: How did the feedback help? How did it feel to give that type of feedback? What worked for you? How might that affect your learning? How does that help you follow our class rules?

Spotlight: The Natural Learning Cycle in Seventh Grade

Mrs. Sullivan stands at the door and welcomes her fourth period seventh grade English students into the classroom. After the final bell, she closes the door and raises her hand, walking to the front of the room. Students finish up their conversations and turn their attention to her. She asks the students to think back to their class meeting last week when they discussed using respectful words and tone with each other, even when they disagree or feel frustrated with each other. Mrs. Sullivan shares a few examples of students using some new strategies during their work earlier this week.

Mrs. Sullivan goes on to share a new goal with her students: "Since you are doing a good job using more respectful words and tone of voice with each other, you are ready to learn a new skill. We are going to focus on offering specific, positive, helpful feedback on each other's work. I'd like you all to learn how to move beyond saying 'I liked it' or 'good job' when commenting on work, and instead provide helpful, constructive feedback."

She turns on her whiteboard projector and shares a table filled with language that might be used when giving feedback. She asks her students to read both columns to themselves.

Mrs. Sullivan asks her students to turn to a partner and share what they notice about the sentences and questions in each column. She then asks her students for ideas about how they might label the two columns. She listens as students offer ideas, and then writes "Instead of saying this . . ." at the top of the left column and "Try saying this . . ." at the top of the right column.

Instead of saying this . . .	Try saying this . . .
"That was good!"	"The beginning of your essay really captured my interest. It made me want to read more."
"You are an amazing writer."	
"I liked your essay. Good job."	"Have you considered adding transitional sentences between paragraphs? That would make your points sound more connected to each other."
"Can you make this more exciting?"	
"Did you proofread this? It needs editing."	"Your essay is organized, and I know exactly how you feel about this topic after reading it."
	"As a reader, your story seems disjointed. I'm not sure of your main points. Can I suggest an idea for how you could reorganize your essay?"

Mrs. Sullivan then asks her students to consider how these two types of language might make a writer feel and how useful the feedback might be. She asks for a volunteer. Malika raises her hand, and Mrs. Sullivan sits next to her and pretends she is giving Malika feedback on her writing. Mrs. Sullivan looks at a piece of Malika's writing and says, "This is so good!" She then looks at the piece of writing again and says, "The beginning of your essay really captured my interest. It made me want to read more." Mrs. Sullivan then asks Malika to share how each piece of feedback made her feel and how helpful she thought each one was.

Mrs. Sullivan then shares the focus for several upcoming classes. "Our goal is to move away from the language in the left column in this chart, and start using the language from the right column when conferencing with each other about your writing." She hands out notecards and asks students to write a phrase they want to stop using when giving feedback, and an example of language they want to start using instead. She asks students to keep the notecards in their writing folders.

Mrs. Sullivan continues with a five-minute minilesson on important keywords to use in an opinion essay. She tells students they have twelve minutes to continue working independently on their writing, and then will have about eight minutes for conferencing with a classmate to receive feedback. When giving feedback, Mrs. Sullivan prompts the students to take out their notecards with their feedback goals and use that to help guide their feedback. She also puts up the table with the types of feedback that were used during goal setting.

After several days of peer conferencing, Mrs. Sullivan leads the class in a reflection about the specific, positive, and helpful types of feedback they were practicing. She asks the class a few open-ended questions, such as "Did anyone find any feedback that was really helpful? Why?" and "How did it feel to give that type of feedback?" She closes the reflection by asking, "How does that type of feedback help you learn more and follow our class rules?"

In these examples, the natural learning cycle is used for students to learn and practice skills that lead to more prosocial behavior—it is not a strategy for responding to misbehavior. The goal is to teach discipline in ways that foster active engagement, so students can construct their own understanding and skill.

Your Own Natural Learning Cycle

Consider the class rules you typically establish with your students. How do students learn about these rules? How do students know what it looks like, sounds like, and feels like to follow the rules? When you observe students struggling to follow the rules, how can they build their own awareness of off-task behavior and following the rules instead of relying on cues from a teacher? The goal is for students to follow the rules even when we are not with them. This comes from repeated goal setting, practice, and reflection.

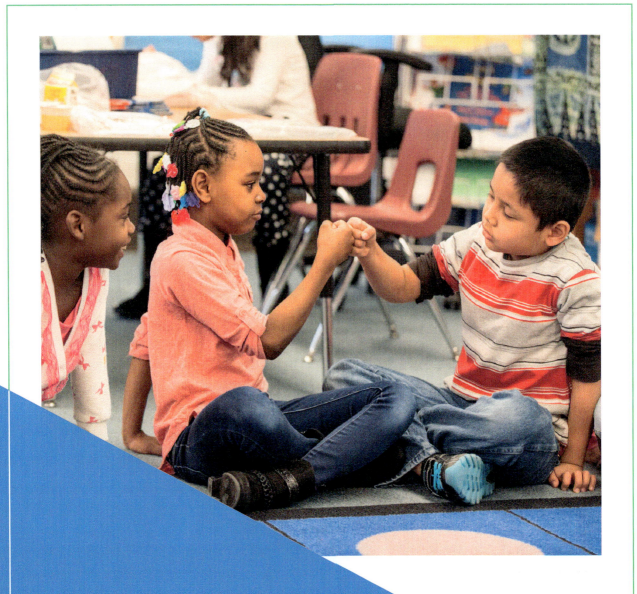

Teaching kids to count is fine, but teaching them what counts is best.

—Bob Talbert

Social and Emotional Learning

The Collaborative for Academic, Social, and Emotional Learning (CASEL) defines social and emotional learning (SEL) as "the process through which all young people and adults acquire and apply the knowledge, skills, and attitudes to develop healthy identities, manage emotions and achieve personal and collective goals, feel and show empathy for others, establish and maintain supportive relationships, and make responsible and caring decisions" (CASEL, n.d.).

The goal of social and emotional learning is for students to acquire the appropriate skills needed to demonstrate developmentally appropriate responses and behaviors in a given situation. To be successful in and out of school, students need to learn a set of social and emotional competencies: cooperation, assertiveness, responsibility, empathy, and self-control. These competencies form the C.A.R.E.S. framework, which has been widely taught to and adopted by educators using the Responsive Classroom approach. These competencies connect to many other essential skills such as speaking and listening, problem-solving, perspective taking, and perseverance.

Cooperation is the ability to:

- Establish new relationships, maintain positive relationships and friendships, and avoid social isolation

- Resolve conflicts and accept differences

- Be a contributing member of the classroom and community in which one lives, works, learns, and plays
- Work productively and collaboratively with others

Assertiveness is the ability to:

- Take initiative
- Stand up for one's ideas without hurting or negating others
- Seek help
- Persevere with a challenging task
- Recognize one's individual self as separate from the environment, circumstances, or conditions one is in

Responsibility is the ability to:

- Motivate oneself to act and follow through on expectations
- Define a problem, consider the consequences, and choose a positive solution

Empathy is the ability to:

- Recognize, appreciate, or understand another's state of mind or emotions
- Be receptive to new ideas and perspectives
- See, appreciate, and value differences and diversity in others

Self-control is the ability to:

- Recognize and regulate one's thoughts, emotions, and behaviors in order to be successful in the moment and remain on a successful trajectory

Social and emotional competence develops over a lifetime. Readiness to demonstrate social and emotional skills in a given situation happens through explicit instruction, with opportunities to practice and prepare, and then to reflect on previous responses. Foundational experiences for SEL help students build and practice both interpersonal and intrapersonal skills that contribute to the creation of a positive learning community. Developmentally appropriate community-building strategies such as Morning Meetings, Responsive Advisory Meetings, energizers, brain breaks, and closing circles help students explore and practice SEL skills each day. (For more details on these community-building strategies, see the appendix, pages 89–90. For more on building a positive community, see Chapter 3.)

What follows are some examples of the natural learning cycle process being used to teach the C.A.R.E.S. competencies.

Grade Level: Kindergarten

SEL Competency: Self-control

1. **Provide a Foundational Experience:** Sharing during Morning Meeting, listeners are invited to ask questions and make comments.

2. **Identify SEL Skill for Growth:** Waiting until the speaker is finished before raising a hand to ask questions or make comments.

3. **Leverage the Natural Learning Cycle:** Throughout the day.

   Goal setting: Interactive Modeling to demonstrate waiting until a speaker is finished before raising hands to ask questions or make comments. Students choose a strategy to try.

   Working: All day, with a check in at midday.

   Reflection: What strategies did you try? What happens when you wait until the speaker is finished to raise your hand to ask questions? What happens when other classmates wait until the end to ask questions? The teacher also shares what they noticed.

Spotlight: Goal Setting

Mrs. Rossi asks her students to gather in a circle on the carpet. "I've noticed that you are remembering to raise your hand and wait to be called on when you have something to say or want to ask a question. That's one way to follow our rule that says to be respectful. It feels respectful to me to not be interrupted when I am speaking. And I've noticed that during sharing in Morning Meeting, you are able to wait until the sharer says they are ready for questions and comments.

"But I've also noticed that during the day, students are raising their hands before I have finished giving directions, while I am still teaching or speaking. Sometimes your hands are waving around for several minutes. I bet your arm gets tired! Although you are following the rules by raising your hand, when you raise your hand before I am finished speaking—especially when I am giving directions or explaining something—it feels disrespectful and it is very distracting. I imagine it can also be distracting you from listening to what I am saying, because you are busy trying to remember your own thoughts or questions."

Mrs. Rossi explains that they are going to work on waiting until the speaker is finished giving directions before raising a hand to ask questions and make comments. Mrs. Rossi uses Interactive Modeling to demonstrate while her students watch. She uses a think-aloud to make her thoughts visible to the students. Mrs. Rossi places her hand on her head to signal that she is sharing her inner thoughts and says, "I have a question right now for my teacher, but she hasn't finished explaining the directions yet. She might even answer my question by the time she's done. I better tune in to her words. I'll keep my hands in my lap for now."

Mrs. Rossi asks students what they noticed about what she did, and then asks a few students to demonstrate the skill as well.

Mrs. Rossi asks her students what they might do with their hands if they feel the urge to put them up while she is speaking. They shared that they could sit on their hands, fold them into fists, or clasp them together and put them in their lap.

Then Mrs. Rossi has everyone practice the skill right away while she gives directions for goal setting. Mrs. Rossi restates the goal: "I want you to remember to save your questions and comments while someone is speaking, and raise your hand to ask a question after the speaker is finished. Choose a strategy for your hands that you want to try today, and imagine the words you might say to yourself."

Grade Level: Second

SEL Competency: Cooperation

1. **Provide a Foundational Experience:** Read-aloud, *Words and Your Heart* by Kate Jane Neal.

2. **Identify SEL Skill for Growth:** Able to make and keep friends by using kind words when interacting with others.

3. **Leverage the Natural Learning Cycle:** Throughout the day.

    Goal setting: Brainstorm kind words/phrases to use, create a list, then choose two to use today.

    Working: All day.

    Reflection: Closing circle reflection: What were some of the kind words you heard today? How did it feel to use kind words today? How did it feel to receive kind words? What are some new kind words we can use tomorrow?

Spotlight: The Natural Learning Cycle in Second Grade

Mrs. Patel notices that she is hearing a lot of unkind words from the second grade students in her class, and that these words are often said with an unfriendly tone of voice. She is worried about the students being able to maintain friendships and a positive sense of community in the classroom. Mrs. Patel decides to begin to address this issue by reading aloud *Words and Your Heart* by Kate Jane Neal. The discussion afterward highlights for students that words have power, and words can affect how others feel.

The next day, Mrs. Patel asks her students a thinking question during the morning message about any kind words they have heard or used recently. At the end of their Morning Meeting, Mrs. Patel asks students to turn to a partner and share their responses to the thinking question. She then asks students to share their ideas aloud, and together they brainstorm a list of kind words they might use with each other in school.

Mrs. Patel asks students to choose two kind sentences to try to use today, then says, "Let's listen carefully for more kind words in our classroom today."

Mrs. Patel posts the list of kind words on the whiteboard at the front of the room. During the day, she watches and listens as students begin using the words from the chart with each other. Several times during the day, Mrs. Patel models the skill by walking over to the chart and then saying something to a student nearby. She uses reinforcing language when she hears a student using kind words: "I bet those words made Lanelle feel really good" and "Did you notice how Malik smiled when you said that to him?"

At the end of the day, during closing circle, Mrs. Patel asks her class some reflection questions, including "What were some of the kind words you heard today? How did it feel to use kind words today? How did it feel to receive kind words?" Mrs. Patel incorporates turn and talks for students to respond to the questions. She closes the reflection with a final question: "What are some new kind words we can use tomorrow?" She adds the kind words to the chart as students share aloud.

After the students leave for the day, Mrs. Patel types up the list of kind words. She writes a short email to the families of her students explaining what they practiced today and shares the list. In the email, she suggests that the students' families could reinforce the use of kind words at home as well.

Kind Words

Thanks for your help.

You are a good partner.

You are nice.

I've noticed how hard you've been trying.

I learned something from you.

You have great ideas.

You are creative.

I am glad we are in the same class.

Your practice is really paying off.

You made me smile.

You bring happiness to our class.

You just made my day better.

Grade Level: Third

SEL Competency: Responsibility

1. **Provide a Foundational Experience:** Role-play making choices.

2. **Identify SEL Skill for Growth:** Making good, thoughtful choices that take care of your needs and the needs of others.

3. **Leverage the Natural Learning Cycle:** Throughout the week.

    Goal setting: Think of times when you need to make a choice. Consider if that choice takes care of what you need while at the same time takes care of others. This is how you make responsible choices. Interactive Modeling lesson about using inner thoughts to debate the pros and cons of choices.

    Working: All week, with a focus on recess.

    Reflection: What have you noticed about the choices you made this week? What changes have you noticed at recess? Is it hard or easy to make choices that take care of what you need while also taking care of others? Why?

Spotlight: Working

Mr. Cohen is hoping that focusing on making good choices this week will help alleviate frequent conflicts between his third graders during recess. When it's time for recess, he reminds them about making good choices that work for everyone before they head out to the playground. Mr. Cohen makes a point to spend a few minutes each day outside during recess, watching and listening to his students on the playground.

Mr. Cohen asks his students some reflection questions about recess each time they return to the classroom after lunch: "How did it go at recess? What issues came up today? How did you resolve them? Did anyone have to make a hard choice today? How did you know your choice was good for you and others, too?" Mr. Cohen invites students to share about making choices during academic lessons as well.

Grade Level: Fourth

SEL Competency: Empathy

1. **Provide a Foundational Experience:** Morning Meeting, Take a Side activity.

2. **Identify SEL Skill for Growth:** Learn that emotions such as fear and trust have a purpose, and be able to recognize fear and trust in others through verbal and nonverbal cues.

3. **Leverage the Natural Learning Cycle:** Throughout the week.

    Goal setting: For the Take a Side activity, ask for their feelings about roller coasters. Share a chart identifying key information about the emotions of trust and fear. During the week practice recognizing trust and fear in others. Write your personal goal in a journal.

    Working: All week. Journaling each day about fear and trust.

    Reflection: A Journal Journey.

Spotlight: The Natural Learning Cycle in Fourth Grade

On Monday, Ms. Garcia leads another round of Take a Side with her fourth graders during Morning Meeting. She shows the class a photo of a huge roller coaster, and asks, "How do you feel about roller coasters? Stand on this side of the circle if you love roller coasters and you feel happy and excited to ride them, and stand on the other side if you do not like roller coasters and you feel nervous and afraid to go on them." Students move to stand on the side of the circle that matches their feelings about roller coasters. Ms. Garcia asks her students to turn and talk with a partner to name some of the ways they show their feelings about roller coasters. "How does your body react? What would I see you doing when you feel those emotions? What might you be saying?" After a few minutes, Ms. Garcia asks a few students to share out their ideas.

Later, after lunch, Ms. Garcia shares a class goal for the week: students are to practice recognizing trust and fear in others. She provides each student with a journal. Ms. Garcia then shares a chart of information about fear and trust with the class. This chart is also on the first page in the student journals.

	Trust	Fear
Purpose	allows us to be vulnerable and bond with others	protects us from harm or danger
Range of emotions	acceptance—trust—admiration	apprehension—fear—terror
Feels like	confident, secure, safe, comfortable	rapid heartbeat, physical or internal trembling, need to fight or run, forebodings
Looks like	calm, relaxed	clenched chest, wide-open eyes, guarded stance

Ms. Garcia reminds the students that the information in the "Feels like" and "Looks like" rows is very similar to what many students shared during the Take a Side roller-coaster activity. Ms. Garcia highlights some information from the chart: "Note that trust and fear have a range. These emotions can be strong or light. Think of an example when you felt just a little trust or fear, or when you felt trust or fear as a very strong emotion. Write about that in your journal. You have five minutes to jot down some ideas about the range of emotions for trust and fear." Ms. Garcia then asks students, "Can someone feel both trust and fear at the same time?" She has students write a response to that question in their journals and follows up by instructing students to jot down a goal for the week: What do they want to look for when noticing fear or trust in others this week? Ms. Garcia shares with students two prompts to complete in their journals:

My goal this week is to notice the range of trust in others by looking for _____ and listening for _____.

My goal this week is to notice the range of fear in others by looking for _____ and listening for _____.

Each day during the week, Ms. Garcia gives students time to write in their journals about noticing trust and fear in others. She suggests some prompts and open-ended questions to shape journal entries:

- Describe what you saw and heard.
- If you recognized that someone was feeling a range of either trust or fear, what did you notice?
- Was the emotion serving a purpose for that person? What might that be?
- Why do you think those emotions surfaced? What was the purpose? Did it help or hinder the student?
- How might that person react to their emotions to achieve a positive experience? How can others support and react to achieve a positive outcome?
- How are emotions and our responses to emotions connected?

During the week Ms. Garcia also highlights expressions of trust or fear when it appears in literature and writing during academic lessons.

At the end of the week, Ms. Garcia leads the class in an activity called a Journal Journey. Students share with a partner how their thinking may have changed or their knowledge or awareness has grown over the course of the week, citing evidence from their journal entries. This then will become the foundation for an essay that students will be assigned the following week.

Grade Level: Eighth

SEL Competency: Assertiveness

1. **Provide a Foundational Experience:** Responsive Advisory Meeting.

   Post the Quote of the Day:
   There are no mistakes, save one: the failure to learn from a mistake.
   —Robert Tripp, musician

   Maître d' Activity:
   - Table for four: What's one positive thing someone might do after making a mistake, and why?

   - Table for three: What might someone do to avoid being too hard on themselves for making a mistake?

   - Table for two: What might someone do to avoid making the same mistake twice?

2. **Identify SEL Skill for Growth:** Persisting through challenge.

3. **Leverage the Natural Learning Cycle:** Throughout the week.

   Goal setting: One aspect of assertiveness is persevering when faced with a challenging task. Envision you have a friend who has always done OK in school, but this year they are struggling in English. Whenever they get stuck with writing, they get very frustrated and give up and stop writing. Using a sticky note, write down one piece of advice you'd give this friend. Post your advice on the bulletin board. Use the advice during the week for yourself. Take one sticky note if you need it.

   Working: Several class periods during the week.

   Reflection: Closing: Reflection question and Quote Corner activity.

Spotlight: Reflection

Mr. Zhang shares with his class an example of how he used the advice on one of the sticky notes. He then asks his class if anyone else used the advice from the sticky notes.

He has students turn to a partner and share. Mr. Zhang then leads his class in a Quote Corner activity. He points out five different quotes that have been posted around the room. He instructs students to count off by fives and then to stand by the quote labeled with their number. He allows students five minutes to talk in their small groups about how the quote relates to their own work or lives. After the discussion, Mr. Zhang asks each group to share with the whole class some ideas from their discussions.

1

Failure is a part of [the] process. You just learn to pick yourself up. And the quicker and more resilient you become, the better you are.
—Michelle Obama

2

Striving for success without hard work is like trying to harvest where you haven't planted.
—David Bly

3

The ultimate measure of a man is not where he stands in moments of comfort and convenience, but where he stands at times of challenge and controversy.
—Martin Luther King Jr.

4

It is impossible to live without failing at something, unless you live so cautiously that you might as well not have lived at all—in which case, you fail by default.
—J. K. Rowling

5

Motivation is what gets you started. Habit is what keeps you going.
—Jim Ryun

Your Own Natural Learning Cycle

Building an awareness of your own social and emotional learning is important for the successful implementation of SEL lessons for students. Reflecting on the strengths and areas for growth in your own social and emotional competence as an adult can help inform your relationships, behaviors, belief systems, and interpersonal and intrapersonal interactions. Focusing on your own SEL competence, understanding, and growth is a key to success for teaching students about SEL. Remember that you are a model for your students.

Consider the strengths and growth areas for social and emotional learning skills in your students. A good resource to aid you when considering strength and growth areas is Chip Wood's *Yardsticks: Child and Adolescent Development Ages 4–14*, which provides a snapshot of typical social and emotional development and will guide you on what to expect at each age and help identify areas where students may need more support. Consider how you can use the natural learning cycle to focus on social and emotional learning, and provide students time and space to practice and develop SEL skills.

One of the challenging aspects of this work is that progress with SEL happens over time, so you may not always see students' SEL advances during their school year with you. But building awareness and understanding, and providing consistent exposure and repeated practice will eventually result in your students' readiness to exhibit age-appropriate SEL skills.

An education is not so much about making a living as making a person.

—Tara Westover

Conclusion

Writing this final chapter symbolizes the completion of my own yearlong natural learning cycle. Upon final reflection, I feel relieved and proud to have reached this milestone. However, I did not feel that way when I began to write this book. I found it overwhelming to attempt to explain the natural learning cycle—something that we do naturally—with words on a page. I spent more time in the first phase than I anticipated, trying to generate ideas and goals. I created several book outlines, attempting each time to find an engaging and purposeful way to share with educators how to implement this important learning process.

In Chapter 2, I wrote how the natural learning cycle is designed for moving back and forth between phases, and that there are times when a student might move backward through the natural learning cycle to reset a goal or redo some work. I found myself cycling through the actively working and reflecting phases over and over while writing each chapter, often checking back with the original goals as I incorporated critical feedback. Frequent reflection helped me make connections between one chapter and the next.

My advice for you is to start small and keep it simple. One of my favorite sayings is "Go slow to go fast." Consider the power of your words as you support your students' learning in all three phases of the natural learning cycle. Be kind to yourself as you try this new learning process and structure with your students. Just as the writing of this book got off to a rocky start, your first implementation of the natural learning cycle may not go according to your plan. Students may become frustrated, or the learning outcomes may not be met. Remember to engage in your own reflection, too. Have patience with yourself and your students as together you develop more competency with the natural learning cycle. Watch for your students' intrinsic motivation to increase. When that occurs, it will be the ultimate indication that the natural learning cycle is being internalized and leveraged effectively by students.

Appendix

Checklists, Rubrics, and Anchor Chart

Personal Narrative Checklist

How my story sounds	Not yet	Starting to	Yes!
I wrote about **one small moment**.	○	○	○
I **stretched** my story out into a beginning, middle, and end.	○	○	○
I added **details** and tried to show the action instead of just telling what happened.	○	○	○
I added dialogue to make my characters come to life.	○	○	○
I wrote a **powerful ending**.	○	○	○

How my story looks	Not yet	Starting to	Yes!
I used **punctuation** at the ends of sentences.	○	○	○
I used **capital letters** at the beginnings of sentences and for proper nouns.	○	○	○
I circled words that were **spelled** incorrectly, and I used my tools to correct them.	○	○	○

Persuasive Essay Checklist

Name: _____

My topic: _____

☐ I clearly state my position in the introduction.
☐ I support each reason with details and evidence.
☐ I stay focused on the topic.
☐ My conclusion summarizes my argument.

Other things I want to make sure I do:

☐ _____
☐ _____
☐ _____

Notes: _____
_____
_____
_____
_____

Adapted from Lynn Bechtel and Kristen Vincent, *The Joyful Classroom: Practical Ways to Engage and Challenge Elementary Students* (2016), page 158.

Persuasive Essay Rubric

Name: _____

Essay Topic: _____

	4 – Advanced	3 – Proficient	2 – Approaching	1 – Beginning
Focus/ topic/ opening	Strongly and clearly states a personal opinion. Introduces the main points of the opinion/argument.	Clearly names the personal opinion. Makes some reference to the main points of the opinion/argument.	Personal opinion is not clearly stated. Makes little or no reference to the main points of the opinion/argument.	Personal opinion is not easily understood. Makes no reference to the main points of the opinion/argument.
Support for position	Includes three or more reasons for the opinion, and each reason is supported by evidence (facts, statistics, examples). The writer addresses potential reader concerns, biases, or arguments and has provided at least one counterargument.	Includes three or more reasons for the opinion, and each reason is supported by evidence (facts, statistics, examples).	Includes two reasons for the opinion and provides minimal evidence for each reason (facts, statistics, examples).	Includes one reason for the opinion but provides little evidence to support the reason.
Transitions	Uses a variety of transitions that clearly show how ideas are connected.	Transitions show how ideas are connected. Uses some variety in transitions.	Some transitions are used; connections between ideas are not clear.	Transitions are unclear or not present.
Closing paragraph	The conclusion leaves the reader clearly understanding the writer's opinion. Author clearly summarizes opinion/argument.	The conclusion leaves the reader understanding the writer's opinion. Author summarizes opinion/argument.	Author is not clear in summarizing opinion/argument.	There is no conclusion.
Grammar and spelling	Contains few if any errors.	Contains few errors and errors do not interfere with meaning.	Contains many errors and errors interfere with meaning.	Contains many errors that interfere with meaning and make essay difficult to understand.

Persuasive Essay Rubric

Name: _____

Essay Topic: _____

Concerns Areas for improvement	**Criteria for Proficient Work**	**Advanced** Evidence of exceeding standards
	Criteria #1: Focus/topic/opening Clearly names the personal opinion. Makes some reference to the main points of the opinion/argument.	
	Criteria #2: Support for position Includes three or more reasons for the opinion, and each reason is supported by evidence (facts, statistics, examples).	
	Criteria #3: Transitions Transitions show how ideas are connected, and some variety of transitions are used.	
	Criteria #4: Closing paragraph The conclusion leaves the reader understanding the writer's opinion. Author summarizes opinion/argument.	
	Criteria #5: Grammar and spelling Contains few errors and errors do not interfere with meaning.	

Adapted from Lynn Bechtel and Kristen Vincent, *The Joyful Classroom: Practical Ways to Engage and Challenge Elementary Students* (2016), page 161.

Anchor Chart

How to Put Events in Order

- Start with a main idea.
- Tell what happened first, second, third, and so on.
- Conclude with what took place last.
- Choose only the most important steps to include.

Adapted from Margaret Berry Wilson, *The Language of Learning: Teaching Students Core Thinking, Listening, and Speaking Skills* (2015), page 112.

Sample Interactive Modeling Plans

How to Clean Up an Area of the Classroom (kindergarten)

Steps	What it might sound like/look like
1. Say what you will model and why.	Teacher: "Our rules say that we will take care of each other and our classroom. When center time ends, those rules mean we carefully clean up. Let's pretend it's the end of center time and I have been playing in the block area. Watch to see how I clean up."
2. Model the behavior.	With kindergartners gathered in the block area, the teacher carefully puts away some blocks that were out on the floor. The teacher checks that each block goes back where it belongs, and scans the area to see if any other blocks are still on the floor. The teacher finds a block that was left behind and puts it away. When the teacher finishes putting all the blocks away, they walk to a student table and sit in a chair.
3. Ask students what they noticed.	"What did you notice about how I followed our rules as I cleaned up the block area?" "How did I make sure all the blocks were in the right place?" "How did I make sure I found all the blocks?"
4. Invite one or more students to model.	The teacher places some blocks back on the floor. "Who wants to show the class what it might look like for partners to clean up the block area?" The teacher chooses two students. "Watch as Tony and Lexi clean up the block area."
5. Again, ask students what they noticed.	"What did you notice about how Lexi and Tony cleaned up the block area?"
6. Have all students practice.	The teacher tells the students that they will have opportunities to practice cleaning up the block area all week. "I'll make sure that everyone gets a chance to practice cleaning up the block area. I'll watch and see how we're doing with that. How will we know if we're taking good care of the blocks?"
7. Provide feedback.	During the week, the teacher makes sure different students clean up the blocks each day, guiding them as needed.

Appendix 85

Using a Hand Lens (second grade)

Steps	What it might sound like/look like
1. Say what you will model and why.	"Today, we'll learn how to use a hand lens, just like scientists do to observe what they're studying. We'll also learn how to carefully record what we see. I want you to know that I'm thinking as I use the lens, so I'll share out loud my thoughts part of the time. Watch to learn what I'm thinking and doing."
2. Model the behavior.	The teacher touches her head with an index finger. "I am using my microphone to share my inner thoughts." The teacher picks up the hand lens and peers through it at a leaf, adjusting its distance from the leaf and her eye. "I see lots of beautiful lines on this leaf. I'll draw the biggest ones first." The teacher carefully sets down the hand lens and picks up a pencil.
3. Ask students what they noticed.	"What did you notice about how I used the lens?" "What did I do with the lens to make sure I could see all the details of the leaf?"
4. Invite one or more students to model.	"Who would like to show us how to carefully use the hand lens to study another leaf?"
5. Again, ask students what they noticed.	"What did you notice about the way José used the hand lens?"
6. Have all students practice.	The teacher distributes hand lenses and a bin of leaves to each table. "You may use a hand lens to observe the leaves on your table. I will be watching to see how you are carefully using the hand lens."
7. Provide feedback.	"Everyone was using the hand lenses carefully to get a good view of the leaves."

Working Independently (fifth grade)

Steps	What it might sound like/look like
1. Say what you will model and why.	"The goal for this year is to be able to work on your own assignments and allow for other classmates to do the same. Watch and see how this table group works on our research."
2. Model the behavior.	The teacher and three students (coached ahead of time) sit at a table in the middle of the classroom and start working intently. After a short time, to show students that some talking about the work is OK during this time, the teacher turns to a student and quietly tells him a fact she just discovered. The student responds, "That's so cool!" in a quiet voice. They then return to their work.
3. Ask students what they noticed.	"What did you notice about how we took care of ourselves and each other?" "Did we talk? What did you notice about how we talked to each other?"
4. Invite one or more students to model.	The teacher chooses four students to demonstrate and asks two of them to have a quick, quiet exchange about something they read.
5. Again, ask students what they noticed.	"What did you notice about the way they were using their independent work time?"
6. Have all students practice.	"Head to your tables and continue your research. We will all practice what independent work looks like."
7. Provide feedback.	"I'm seeing everyone focused on their work. I can hear brief, quiet conversations about your research. That kind of focus will really help us learn a lot this year!"

Turning in Homework (seventh grade)	
Steps	**What it might sound like/look like**
1. Say what you will model and why.	"Today, I'll show you the procedure for turning in homework. Watch what I do."
2. Model while students notice.	The teacher silently demonstrates the process of placing an assignment into the bin labeled Homework. "What did you notice about how I turned in my assignment?"
3. Give students the opportunity to collaborate and practice.	"Now you will practice how to hand in your homework using the writing assignment from your English folder."
4. Reinforce the practice with immediate feedback.	"I see students taking out their assignments before they go up to the bin." "I notice students carefully placing their assignment on the top of the pile of papers. It looks like we'll be organized and ready to learn because everyone has carefully handed in their work."

Adapted from Ellie Cornecelli and Amber Searles, *Building an Academic Community: The Middle School Teacher's Guide to the First Four Weeks of the School Year* (2018), page 37.

Community-Building Strategies

Morning Meeting is a twenty-to-thirty-minute whole-class gathering at the beginning of each day that is used to set the tone for engaged learning, create positive community, and reinforce academic and social and emotional skills in lively ways.

Morning Meeting consists of four sequential components:

1. **Greeting.** Students greet each other by name and may also shake hands, sing or chant, and do fun movements.

2. **Sharing.** Students share some news or information about themselves or their learning and respond to each other's sharing.

3. **Group activity.** The whole class does a short, inclusive group activity that can reinforce learning and build class cohesion through active participation.

4. **Morning message.** Students practice academic skills and warm up for the day by reading and discussing a daily note to the class posted by the teacher.

Responsive Advisory Meeting connects a teacher (the advisor) with a group of middle school students (the advisees) to provide academic and social-emotional support and to strengthen the school community. Responsive Advisory Meeting has a predictable structure, and each meeting is organized around a distinct purpose that underlies the meeting's topic and activities.

The four components of Responsive Advisory Meeting are:

1. **Arrival welcome.** The advisor welcomes each student by name as they enter the classroom.

2. **Announcements.** In advance, the advisor writes an interactive message and displays it where it can be easily seen and read by all students.

3. **Acknowledgments.** In pairs or small groups, students share their responses to a prompt in the announcements message, a piece of news about themselves, or ideas about a topic related to their studies or interests.

4. **Activity.** The whole group does a fun, lively activity that's focused on the specific purpose of the meeting.

Energizers and brain breaks are quick, whole-class activities that can be done any time in the school day to give students a mental and physical break from academic work. They can be lively or calming, have an academic component or not. They can be used to transition students between learning activities, as a pick-me-up during intensive lessons, or as a way to keep order during waiting times.

Closing circle is a five- to- ten-minute gathering that consists of a group activity or two to bring the school day to a positive, peaceful end. In a closing circle, students might reflect on the learning that day or week, and then celebrate together with a song or cheer. Closing circles build trust and cooperation and foster positive energy and attitudes in both students and teachers.

References

Anderson, Mike. 2019. *What We Say and How We Say It Matter: Teacher Talk That Improves Student Learning and Behavior*. Alexandria, VA: Association for Supervision and Curriculum Development.

Beard, Colin, and John P. Wilson. 2006. *Experiential Learning: A Best Practice Handbook for Educators and Trainers*. 2nd ed. Philadelphia: Kogan Page.

Center for Responsive Schools. 2016. *The Power of Our Words for Middle School: Teacher Language That Helps Students Learn*. Turners Falls, MA: Center for Responsive Schools.

Center for Responsive Schools. 2018a. "Know Your Students: Developmentally Responsive Planning." https://www.responsiveclassroom.org/know-students-developmentally-responsive-planning/.

Center for Responsive Schools. 2018b. *Teaching Self-Discipline: The Responsive Classroom Guide to Helping Students Dream, Behave, and Achieve in Elementary School*. Turners Falls, MA: Center for Responsive Schools.

Collaborative for Academic, Social, and Emotional Learning (CASEL). n.d. "What Is SEL?" https://casel.org/what-is-sel/.

Covington, Martin V. 2000. "Goal Theory, Motivation, and School Achievement: An Integrative Review." *Annual Review of Psychology* 51 (1): 171–200. https://doi.org/10.1146/annurev.psych.51.1.171.

Deci, Edward, with Richard Flaste. 1995. *Why We Do What We Do: Understanding Self-Motivation*. New York: Penguin Books.

Degen, Ronald Jean. 2011. "Brain-Based Learning: The Neurological Findings About the Human Brain That Every Teacher Should Know to Be Effective." Working Paper 77/2011, Polytechnic Institute of Leiria, Leiria, Portugal.

Denton, Paula. 2013. *The Power of Our Words: Teacher Language That Helps Children Learn*. 2nd ed. Turners Falls, MA: Center for Responsive Schools.

Dewey, John. 1938/1963. *Experience and Education*. New York: Collier MacMillan.

Kolb, Alice Y., and David A. Kolb. 2008. "The Learning Way: Meta-cognitive Aspects of Experiential Learning." *Simulation and Gaming: An Interdisciplinary Journal of Theory, Practice and Research* 40 (3): 297–327. https://doi.org/10.1177/1046878108325713.

Kolb, Alice Y., David A. Kolb, Angela Passarelli, and Garima Sharma. 2014. "On Becoming an Experiential Educator: The Educator Role Profile." *Simulation and Gaming: An Interdisciplinary Journal of Theory, Practice and Research* 45 (2): 204–234. https://doi.org/10.1177%2F1046878114534383.

Meehan, Caitie. 2016. "Making Learning Meaningful: It's All About the Why." Center for Responsive Schools. https://www.responsiveclassroom.org/making-learning-meaningful-its-all-about-the-why/.

Moon, Jennifer A. 2004. *A Handbook of Reflective and Experiential Learning: Theory and Practice*. London: Routledge.

Morris, Thomas Howard. 2019. "Experiential Learning—A Systematic Review and Revision of Kolb's Model." *Interactive Learning Environments* 28 (8): 1064–77. https://doi.org/10.1080/10494820.2019.1570279.

Piaget, Jean. 1923/1959. *The Language and Thought of the Child*. New York: Humanities Press.

Pink, Daniel. 2009. *Drive: The Surprising Truth About What Motivates Us.* New York: Riverhead Books.

Wood, Chip. 2017. *Yardsticks: Child and Adolescent Development Ages 4–14.* 4th ed. Turners Falls, MA: Center for Responsive Schools.

Zull, James E. 2002. *The Art of Changing the Brain: Enriching the Practice of Teaching by Exploring the Biology of Learning.* Sterling, VA: Stylus.

Zull, James E. 2012. *From Brain to Mind: Using Neuroscience to Guide Change in Education.* Sterling, VA: Stylus.

Suggested Readings

Anderson, Mike. 2019. *What We Say and How We Say It Matter: Teacher Talk That Improves Student Learning and Behavior.* Alexandria, VA: Association for Supervision and Curriculum Development.

Center for Responsive Schools. 2016. *The Joyful Classroom: Practical Ways to Engage and Challenge Elementary Students.* Turners Falls, MA: Center for Responsive Schools.

Center for Responsive Schools. 2016. *The Power of Our Words for Middle School: Teacher Language That Helps Children Learn.* Turners Falls, MA: Center for Responsive Schools.

Center for Responsive Schools. 2018. *Building an Academic Community: The Middle School Teacher's Guide to the First Four Weeks of the School Year.* Turners Falls, MA: Center for Responsive Schools.

Center for Responsive Schools. 2018. *The Responsive Advisory Meeting Book: 150+ Purposeful Plans for Middle School.* Turners Falls, MA: Center for Responsive Schools.

Center for Responsive Schools. 2018. *Teaching Self-Discipline: The Responsive Classroom® Guide to Helping Students Dream, Behave, and Achieve in Elementary School.* Turners Falls, MA: Center for Responsive Schools.

Center for Responsive Schools. 2019. *Seeing the Good in Students: A Guide to Classroom Discipline in Middle School.* Turners Falls, MA: Center for Responsive Schools.

Deci, Edward, with Richard Flaste. 1996. *Why We Do What We Do: Understanding Self-Motivation.* New York: Penguin Books.

Denton, Paula. 2015. *The Power of Our Words: Teacher Language That Helps Children Learn.* 2nd ed. Turners Falls, MA: Center for Responsive Schools.

Dweck, Carol S. 2007. *Mindset: The New Psychology of Success*. Updated ed. New York: Ballantine Books.

Kriete, Roxann, and Carol Davis. 2016. *The Morning Meeting Book K–8*. 3rd ed. Turners Falls, MA: Center for Responsive Schools.

Pink, Daniel H. 2011. *Drive: The Surprising Truth About What Motivates Us*. New York: Riverhead Books.

Wilson, Margaret Berry. 2015. *The Language of Learning: Teaching Students Core Thinking, Listening, and Speaking Skills*. Turners Falls, MA: Center for Responsive Schools.

Wilson, Margaret Berry. 2016. *Interactive Modeling: A Powerful Technique for Teaching Children*. Turners Falls, MA: Center for Responsive Schools.

Wood, Chip. 2017. *Yardsticks: Children in the Classroom Ages 4–14*. 4th ed. Turners Falls, MA: Center for Responsive Schools.

About the Author

Kristen Vincent is the assistant director of marketing for Center for Responsive Schools and a certified *Responsive Classroom* consulting teacher. Kristen began her teaching career as an educator at the New England Aquarium in Boston, Massachusetts, and taught fourth grade in Needham, Massachusetts. Kristen is the coauthor of *Closing Circles: 50 Activities for Ending the Day in a Positive Way* and *The Joyful Classroom: Practical Ways to Engage and Challenge Elementary Students*, and has authored many articles and blogs for the *Responsive Classroom* website. Kristen currently lives in Westborough, Massachusetts, with her daughter.

About the Publisher

Center for Responsive Schools, Inc., a not-for-profit educational organization, offers professional development, curriculum, and books and resources to support academic, social, and emotional learning.

Center for Responsive Schools (CRS) is the developer of *Responsive Classroom*®, a research-based education approach associated with greater teacher effectiveness, higher student achievement, and improved school climate, and of Fly Five, a comprehensive social-emotional learning curriculum for kindergarten through eighth grade.

CRS Publishing, the independent publishing arm of Center for Responsive Schools, creates inspiring yet practical books for educators and students to support growth, learning, and success in and out of school.

Center for Responsive Schools' vision is to influence and inspire a world-class education for every student in every school, every day, and to bring hope and joy to educators and students alike. Visit us at crslearn.org to learn more: